Trusting you will be
blessed and comforted.

Kathy ⚬

overcoming the

loss of a loved one

GRIEF

Kathy O'Brien

Authentic

First published 2004 by Authentic Media, 9 Holdom Avenue,
Bletchley, Milton Keynes, MK1 1QR, UK and
P.O. Box 1047, Waynesboro, GA 30830-2047, USA.

British Library Cataloguing in Publication Data
A catalogue record for this book is available from the
British Library

1-86024-463-7

Cover design by David Lund
Print Management by Adare Carwin
Printed and Bound in Denmark by Nørhaven Paperback

Acknowledgements

To Geoff – who always knew I'd write a book and encouraged me every step of the way. You'd have smiled at the irony!

To Joy – true, lasting friendship like ours is a most treasured gift; thank you for everything, for always being there and for making me laugh through the tears.

To Mummy and Eddie – I don't know what I would have done without all your support.

To all the other people who helped me 'get through'.

And above all

To God, my Friend, Father, Comforter and every reason for living.

THANK YOU

Contents

Chapter 1

When IT Happens

I thought I'd know
Sense tearing
Yet I was blissfully unaware
Until that knock
That set my heart on fire
In one instant
One millisecond
I knew
That I knew, the depths of hell's grip
On my heart
A terror so deep
It traumatised every fibre of my 3-fold being
Plunging me to a darkness never dreamt of
Never imagined in my darkest nightmares
Oh how my heart aches
For the love of my beloved.

K.S. O'Brien

They woke me at 4 a.m. In the dimly lit room my eyes tried to focus, as my muddled brain fought into consciousness. What was this dragging feeling in my stomach? Why did I feel so wretched? Then I remembered. They were waking me – to watch my father die.

I'd been given a side ward at the hospital. Overcome by exhaustion, unable to continue watching and waiting, I'd slept, only on the proviso they'd wake me before he died. I was twenty-seven, married just two years, totally unprepared and very, very scared.

Only thirty-six hours previously, this man, who had recently completed a marathon walk, was seemingly fit and well – but now I was standing by his bed waiting for his last breath. And I was scared to the very pit of my stomach. I'd never expected the first person I saw die to be my own father and nothing had prepared me for this: not attending funerals, not even being with my father-in-law a few hours before he died. Nothing had prepared me to stand by and watch as my father left this world behind, with a final sigh! This man who had loved me from the moment I'd been born and throughout my life, was dead.

❦

Eleven years later, I was equally unprepared: unprepared for the policeman's knock on the door; the horror; the shock and another sudden death. But this time the man I loved most in the whole world, my husband, was already laid out in the morgue for me to identify. 10 o'clock at night. No one should have to do that. Not then – not ever.

Because nothing prepares us for the trauma that is death. Whether it's expected, as in my father-in-law's death after five years of dementia, or sudden death as with my husband killed in a road traffic accident, or my father after swift illness – nothing prepares us.

Death literally tears us apart. It rips into us physically (oh yes, it's not just emotional pain) and then it spits us out, to crawl as best we can, back to life – a life that often we barely recognise, at least in the beginning.

So, if we can't prepare, how can we possibly cope, survive and more than that, emerge from grief whole? Is it in fact possible at all? And how, as Christians, should we respond? Should we embrace death or fight it all the way? And how can we best help someone who's bereaved or facing imminent bereavement?

The aim of this book is to provide pointers along the way: signposts through the journey both for the bereaved and others involved. I don't come from a position of knowing all about the 'stages of grief'.

Having said that, there are recognised phases we all pass through when grieving. There's the initial shock, a sense of unreality which allows us to function in the immediate aftermath. Then there's disbelief tied up with that shock, often followed by anger. The length of time each stage lasts varies individual by individual. Anger can move into a period of depression, which is also a natural part of the grief process, before emerging into a stage of acceptance and readiness to move forward.

However, I don't have a professional background as a grief counsellor. I come instead from a place of personal experience. One thing I will say, right from the start, is that everyone's walk through grief is different. My experience of grief was different when I lost my father, from when I miscarried, from when my husband died.

You will find your own way through and you will find God in the midst of your very darkest hour, if you look for him. There will be lows, there will be some highs but throughout, the everlasting arms will be underneath you. Sometimes you'll be aware of them, other times you won't.

❦

I guess my life into young adulthood was pretty normal for someone growing up in a Western culture. I was shielded from death and the dying. The people I'd known who died were all elderly: 'they lived a good life'; 'they were ready to go'; 'they're out of pain and at peace now' were platitudes I just swallowed and accepted, even repeated – all without thinking. It was only when death cut directly across my expectations that I sat up and took notice. Let's be frank here, neither you nor I expect to die young. Somewhere deep in our psyche we expect to live to a ripe old age. We might never have voiced this belief, but deep down it's there. We seem to be born with an innate sense that we have a 'right' to a full span of years. Likewise, we expect those we love to live long lives too: 'after all he never really harmed anyone'; 'he was such a good person'; 'he didn't deserve this pain.' Especially if we're Christians, we know that God's blessing includes long life, three score years and ten (or more, we silently add, as people live longer nowadays). When someone is sick we earnestly pray for their healing (as indeed we should) and we fight death right to the end.

And why?

Before we go into these questions, let's back up a moment.

You've probably picked up this book because somebody close to you has died or is dying. Maybe someone you love very dearly. From across the pages I want to pause and say, 'I'm sorry'. I'm sorry for your loss. I'm sorry for your pain and I acknowledge that you are hurting, maybe more than you ever thought possible to experience and survive. As I write these words, I pray that the Comforter, the Holy Spirit, will come to you and minister to you, right where you are. For in this dark time, you have a marvellous opportunity, though it might not feel like it right now. But you have the chance to come right into the closeness of God's comfort, to truly experience his presence, as you walk through the 'valley of the shadow of death'. For in this dark time, he longs to bring his comfort to you when you cry out to him. He longs to draw near.

Maybe you want to help a person who has lost some-one. Equally, this book is for you.

So, your loved one is dead and you are left behind. Perhaps you have known they were dying and you pre-pared as much as anyone can. 'I love yous' and 'good-byes' were said and now they're dead and you are hurt-ing. How can you possibly go on? 'Stop the world! I want to get off!' you silently scream and you might really mean it.

Instead, exactly the opposite happens. Suddenly, it all gets extremely busy. There's a multitude of things that have to be done, right now, and everybody's wanting you to make the decisions.

That First Week

If you've not experienced this before you might be taken totally unawares by the practicalities following a death. This list represents some of the things which need to be considered and I'd encourage you to delegate these as much as you possibly can.

- Notifying family.
- Notifying friends.
- Notifying employers.
- Notifying banks, building societies.

- Getting a copy of the death certificate (get at least six photocopies, you'll need them).
- Registering the death.
- Contacting a funeral director.
- Preparing the funeral.
- Letting people know about the funeral and/or thanksgiving service.
- Dealing with telephone calls of condolence.
- Dealing with visitors (and *their* discomfort).
- Having the house full of people wanting to help, but not always knowing how.
- Getting used to hearing the name of your loved one in the past tense and having to explain they are dead.
- Contacting solicitors about the estate and a will/probate.
- Dealing with the police if it's a sudden death.
- Coping with post which comes addressed to that person.
- Changing the answerphone message, if their voice is on it.

Hopefully, you will have people around you. You may not. If you do have people offering you help, consider it seriously. You want to get through this and emerge as whole as possible. They want to help. Let them. This support might not be there long-term. Make the most of it whilst it is there and people are thoughtful of your pain – even if you just want to hide away.

Whilst people desperately want to help you, they will probably be feeling at a loss to know how. Odd though it sounds, you will have to help them by stating your needs. Even though decisions are hard to make, may seem 'trite' or too 'final', these will still have to be done.

Tip: For the bereaved and others:
Here are some practical ways people can help.

- Ringing people to let them know.
- Cooking meals and shopping for food. (I found food shopping one of the most painful experiences of all. I could only think of how much I'd shopped for food my husband liked. Supermarkets were a 'no go' place for many weeks.)
- Looking after children or pets' needs.
- Housework, even basic cleaning and laundry.
- Arranging flowers people have sent.
- Deflecting unhelpful callers sensitively.
- Creating space for rest by shielding you (you may feel too exhausted).
- Listening to you and letting you talk about the person who's died.
- Accompanying you to the funeral directors/registry office to certify the death.
- Setting up an administrative file to accumulate all the correspondence (keep it in one central place).
- Photocopying death certificates.
- Word processing a general letter of notification to service providers e.g. gas/electricity/ phone, banks.
- Just being in the house whilst you sleep, so you don't wake to an empty house.
- Ensuring enough supplies of milk, tea, coffee and biscuits for all the people who pop by.

Saying 'Goodbye'

Viewing a person's body used to be a normal thing to do. The dead person was laid out in the front parlour and people could come and 'pay their respects'. This is no longer usually done. The body is removed to the funeral home. However, the need to say 'goodbye' is still strong. It's a matter entirely of individual choice and you will be bombarded by conflicting advice. Should you or should you not view the dead body? I suggest you are the only person who can make that decision.

If you're worried about going to say 'goodbye' because you think that final visit will be the only way you'll remember the person, I'd like to reassure you. More often than not, this last image is swiftly replaced by more pleasant memories of the person when they were alive and the more you focus on this, the easier it becomes.

However, viewing the dead person really can help with coming to terms with the finality of death. There's a real sense that all that's left is a shell, the essence of the person is no longer there.

Funeral directors are usually very co-operative if friends or relatives wish to visit the body and it's straightforward to arrange.

The Funeral

Some of the things I've mentioned need to be set in motion quite swiftly after death, others within the first two weeks.

However, sensitive professionals come into their own during this time. A kind undertaker will lead you through the arrangements and answer your questions.

I felt the undertaker for my husband's funeral became a friend after a few short hours together. His sensitivity helped me face the realities of the final arrangements. His gentle manner brought a sense of order into my chaotic, spinning world. He helped me face that first week, leading up to the funeral. I thank him.

> **Tip:** *If you're not sure which company to use, the local Church of England vicar or your own minister will be able to advise you.*

With the undertaker you'll be able to decide what kind of memorial will suit you best. I opted for a funeral service at the crematorium which was more intimate, followed by a thanksgiving service. I chose this way round so that I had faced the really difficult part first. It wasn't then hanging over me when I had to face the larger group of people at the Thanksgiving Service.

> **Tip:** *When choosing music, be careful. Be warned. I chose a very popular song that meant a huge amount to us. However, it's so popular it was played endlessly on the radio, in supermarkets, even on the 'on-hold' telephone music for my bank. Even now, years later, it can reduce me to tears in a few seconds.*

The first service was my private 'goodbye' to my husband, witnessed by God. I spent most of it in prayer, worshipping, crying, unaware of those around me. Even though I knew it was going to happen, I nearly missed the curtains going around the coffin. It sounds like a silly worry but I found it a most significant point (as was the point during my father's funeral where the coffin descended into the ground), that very last moment of saying 'goodbye' to my husband's physical body, whose every nuances I knew so well. I know if I'd missed it, I would have wanted to run up to the front and grab the curtains back, simply to hold on for another few moments. But of course, I wouldn't have because I'm British and we're supposed to be reserved, aren't we! Instead the regret would have been there and *we are in the business, in this book, of minimising regrets.*

It is part of our protective mechanism to feel numb and people can feel no emotion during a funeral. This can be misconstrued as 'courage' or 'strength'. Whatever, be true to yourself. If you need to cry, what better place! If you can't or don't want to, that's fine too. Don't feel guilty or that you 'ought' to behave in any particular manner. This just adds unnecessary pressure.

> *Tip: I was given a beautiful gift box of tissues. I carried these around with me, as I needed them. A thoughtful and practical gift.*

Afterwards

If you've not been to a funeral, afterwards it's normal for the bereaved to talk to those attending who file past offering condolences. Hard though it is, some will know what to say and bring words of comfort. I remember very little of all this except holding closely onto my friends and family.

> *Tip: If you're attending a funeral and offering condolences, a simple and effective thing is to personalise them.*
> *E.g. I really appreciated his kindness to me.*
> *He had a beautiful smile.*
> *I'm glad she was my friend.*
> *Everyone respected him as a man of integrity at work.*
> *Knowing her enriched my life.*

> *Such personalised condolences bring much comfort and are remembered long after the 'I'm so sorry for your loss' lines, which trip out because we don't quite know what to say.*
>
> *Personalise it. Say something about the person who has died and use their name. The same applies if you are writing a condolence card – do try to include a specific memory of how that person touched your life. These cards will be re-read and often treasured for the comfort they bring, sometimes years down the line.*

Thanksgiving/Memorial Service

I chose to hold this on the same day (with a brief rest and refreshments in between) as many had travelled from other parts of the country and wished to attend both services.

This was a different type of remembering and was more public. Friends and family shared memories and gave tribute. Again, I can recall the personal mentions – the real ones, which acknowledged my husband as a man, not as a perfect icon, but were truthful and sincere.

> *Tip: If you are asked to speak:*
> *If you're giving a tribute keep it short but genuine. Don't try to sum up the whole life of a person. Keep it succinct but relevant, maybe focusing on only one or two particularly special memories.*
>
> *Some of the closest friends and family will be too upset to face this ordeal. One way to say it without having to stand up front, is to write out what you want to say beforehand. Another person, perhaps the minister or someone less emotionally involved, can read it on your behalf.*

There was thanksgiving for our time together interspersed with songs of worship. I felt the support of those present and of God himself.

There was even a moment of intense glee. It struck me that my husband, who was always late for everything, had actually arrived somewhere before me – he'd jumped into eternity and was face-to-face with Jesus. It became a private joke between me and one of our closest friends who knew us both well.

Surprised? So was I – surprised that I could experience joy and laugh, even during that first week. And that's the paradox of death and of a Christian death in particular. I was suffering the deepest grief I'd ever experienced and yet intermingled were what can only be described as flashes of supernatural joy.

One source of amusement was the endless purple and yellow flower arrangements which kept arriving. I love colour. However, some of the arrangement structures were unbelievably rigid and I just had to dismantle them and rearrange them because the flowers themselves were so beautiful. Eventually, when another bouquet arrived, my friend, Joy, and I just laughed knowing it was bound to be purple and yellow – the florists' obvious colour combination for that year. These flashes occurred many times in the early days and were a deep source of joy and subsequently of strength. They occurred during worship at the thanksgiving service; when dear friends arrived at my house for the funeral (it felt like a birthday party, only he was absent); and I also felt it when I discovered a recording of my husband's voice and guitar playing.

This supernatural joy, birthed I believe from friends' prayers, did sustain me.

> *Tip: For the bereaved person:*
> *You might consider writing a love letter to your loved one, expressing your thanks and love for them.*

I handmade a personalised card as a final love-letter to my husband. I thanked him for our years together, chatting about the people he'd be meeting in heaven and the knowledge that we would once again be reunited. (That veil between earth and heaven becomes very thin during bereavement. Eternity for the Christian is suddenly a reality.)

It was particularly helpful for me to be able to say 'until we meet again' and 'goodbye' to this temporal realm. Whilst we didn't have any unfinished business, we might have had, in which case I would have written and asked his forgiveness, voicing any regrets. Remember, we are in the business of minimising regrets as soon as they arise.

Regrets can be rather like a dormant seed. If it doesn't receive the right conditions it doesn't grow. However, if the regrets are not dealt with, replaying them in your head will cause that seed to germinate, put down roots which then become difficult to dislodge. Be rigorous. Deal with regrets, face them head-on. Don't give them a chance to grow.

> *Tip: For someone helping:*
> *You may look at this person and think they've very much 'got it together'. However, it is worth remembering this is the beginning of a long road. The worst might yet be to come for them and you just cannot assume what is going on beneath the surface.*

By the way, I wore a raspberry red skirt and blouse, under my dark grey jacket, to Geoff's funeral. I felt it represented much more of what was happening to me than black would have done and he would have appreciated it. Why red? Geoff loved me in this colour and it represented my broken heart but also my desire to go on living. Somehow it reminded me of Jesus' sacrifice and his sharing in my suffering. I hope it didn't offend anyone, but if it did I really didn't care. I had to get through that day in the way I could. This helped.

You might find something equally significant for you. I recently attended a funeral where people were asked to wear something yellow as it was the dead person's favourite colour.

After the Funeral

Sometimes what's called a 'wake' or gathering where refreshments are served is organised. You may consider not having it at your home but in a church hall and having someone who's not involved in the funeral arrange it. Neighbours or church members are possibilities. This means you can get away when you need to and your home remains a private sanctuary.

Also, be careful not to end up with a house full of guests overnight that you feel obliged to entertain and feed. Close friends and family will be supportive and look after their own needs and yours. You might consider doing something very normal after the funeral is over – it's not irreverent. From what I remember we sat and watched a movie, needing to relax after a very draining day. Conserving your strength will be important as you face the days ahead.

Prayer

God who sees the tears
Wipe away our grief
By the presence of your love.
Where words do not count
Hear the cries of our hearts
And hold our pain
Until it heals.

K.S. O'Brien

Chapter 2

Tears That Won't Stop

Your name is an unspoken utterance
Forever filling my mind
With sighs of longing
Oh, the pause
As I jolt back to the reality
That longing
Is not truth or even actuality
It is just that
Longing
For something so unattainable
That the ache threatens
To crack my heart
In abandonment
Of grief
Where no tears can
Salve the wound
Of never.

K.S. O'Brien

Shock is a terrible thing but an amazingly protective shield. It can block the immediacy of a situation so we can function or cope on some level.

I remember the shock following my husband's death very vividly. In one part it manifested physically – as a creeping sensation all over my skin, a cold sweat and a shot of searing panic. That lasted three full days but was re-visited instantly up to a year later if I so much as thought of the policeman's knock on the door. I learnt to be very strict with my inner thoughts. That element was ghastly.

However, to an extent there was a numbing effect. For some days I existed in a suspended dream-like state, almost observing events and people as an outsider looking in. That state allowed my mind to catch up with what was happening and my emotions a short breathing space. But it didn't last, thankfully – because whilst it put me onto automatic pilot, it was extremely unpleasant especially physically. And when it passed the tears came more often.

Now obviously, I am one person and I share from my own experiences of grief. You are different. Probably men and women respond differently too. But for me, tears came freely and often and many times in inappropriate places.

Looking back, I realise there were different levels of tears. There were the initial tears – sobs that seemed to be wrenched out of the pit of my stomach and shake my whole body. Huge, gulping cries – the anguish of an injured animal. These occurred very often in the early days and I'd find myself curled up with my back against a wall, trying to make myself as small as possible.

> **Tip:** *Nobody could actually alleviate the pain of this type of crying but another person's presence did make it less desperate. Sometimes, to be held in a gentle hug during this terrible phase provides comfort. It's hard for the other person, as they will feel helpless and maybe scared by the depth of your anguish, but just being there is helping.*

I found this kind of devastating crying was expressed in the very early days in particular. Episodes lessened and became infrequent. However, I will be honest here, as it took me totally by surprise, when three years on I suddenly found myself back in this place.

It was the night before I was due to go into hospital for an operation (the third in three years and the second major one since Geoff died). I was scared. I was alone and I'd let my defences down. Self-pity flooded in and all the 'woe is me – what a dreadful lot I've been given' thoughts swirled in my mind. These negative emotions isolated and immobilised me. I couldn't reach out and ask for help. I felt beyond help. And God! Where was God? I certainly didn't turn to him.

The result? I ended up reliving it all – the nightmare of those first hours and the worst of all that followed and I sank into this pit of despair. Isolation and utter abandonment were all I could feel and a searing pain as I sobbed from the depth of my being, 'Where are you, God?'

It was a salutary lesson. Within a few moments my phone rang – a Christian neighbour had heard me howling. Did I want her to come round?

We didn't know each other well but I ended up splurging all my worries, fears, depression, anxiety and doubt over her and she just listened, with kindness and detachment. She didn't try to provide answers or trite statements. She just shared in my pain. And it lessened.

That was a valuable lesson to me. Whilst I know, three years down the line, I am whole and living a new life – I do have a large scar remaining because of what I've experienced. If I'm not very careful and kind to myself, that old wound can be reopened. I have to choose to accept help and to ask for it when I'm so low. (It is truly more blessed to give than to receive – we all prefer to be the giver, don't we?) I had to learn to ask for prayer to deflect any attack of the enemy, because he will kick the boot in when we are flat on our faces, already defeated. He has no rules except to demolish our Christian faith and turn us away from the very source of our life, Jesus. Think I'm exaggerating? I'm not! 'Your enemy the devil prowls around like a roaring lion looking for someone to devour' (1 Peter 5:8); 'The thief comes only to steal and kill and destroy' (John 10:10). If we're weak, he will try to pick us off. If we're isolated and traumatised he will hone in on us – unless we are covered in prayer.

Tip: Wanting to help someone? Pray for the bereaved. In the early days, yours and many others' prayers will buoy them up. But down the months and years, if they pop into your mind, pray for them then and there. That prayer might be the very spiritual protection they need at that moment. Pray that God will command his angels concerning them to protect them in all their ways (Psalm 91:11). Pray that they will be strengthened in their inner being (Ephesians 3:16). Pray that God will be their refuge and fortress. (Psalm 91:2). Resist the enemy on their behalf (Ephesians 6:10–18; 1 Peter 5:9) and pray that their 'feeble hands' and 'the knees that give way' will be steadied, along with their 'fearful hearts' being strengthened (Isaiah 35:3,4).

Drop them a note, an email or a phone call to let them know you prayed for them today. That small act of kindness might be all it takes to rekindle hope and a communication bridge for them to ask for help in the future. Don't assume because they have close friends

> *or family that these needs are being met. Even if they are receiving support, no one ever had too much.*
>
> *Remember, love is kind (1 Corinthians 13:4). Even if it's a year or so since someone was bereaved it doesn't mean they are totally through their grief and not still hitting rough patches. Outward appearances can be deceptive, even to the bereaved person themselves – like me, they can be caught by surprise when grief pops up again. It can be very hard at that stage to ask for help – new people might be in our lives who've never even known our former life.*

So, back to the tears. Once the sobbing, the convulsive tears, subside a different type of crying can emerge. Whilst the first brings relief and a washing of the pain – almost like a pressure valve being released – I found the next type of crying was very different.

These were the tears I would try to resist starting. That might sound odd but once they started they wouldn't stop. They were the quieter tears of desperation. They were the tears, not of an animal in physical pain but in terrible emotional and psychological pain. And these whimpering tears were fickle. They'd start unexpectedly and could catch me without warning.

I'd be unable to sleep, maybe sitting looking at photos of my husband, and they'd start. Sparked by a memory, often a happy one, these tears came from the well of a broken heart, lost dreams and disappointment. When they started they'd trickle at first but soon build up to full flow – but still, often quietly. They could go on for hours but they didn't help. They brought no relief.

They might turn up in the depths of the night, or walking down the street, or even in a supermarket – which

totally embarrassed me. Shopping was always a mine-
field because the music would trigger things. I have
mentioned before that I had a special song played at
Geoff's funeral. This particular song became 'our song'
just before Geoff died. It was representative of our love
and its strength. However, it was very popular and
played endlessly in shops in the months following his
death (and even on phone calls when waiting for service). The unexpectedness meant I wasn't prepared and
the music sliced through to my grief, demolishing my
protective defences. Tears would start and often I'd have
to leave hurriedly or I'd want to just stand and shout:
'My husband's dead!' as if I needed others to acknowledge my horror – needing recognition that the world had
changed, because no one else was behaving any differently. Of course, I never followed through on these
impulses but they were a strong part of the emotional
turmoil. Embarrassingly and awkwardly, this would
happen in church more than anywhere else. The worship, whether conventional or free, would demolish my
defences. The rawness of the angry wound would be
exposed and the pain, along with my desperate longing
for God's comfort, would overwhelm me. Tears would
come, often uncontrollably and with desperation; a combination of crying out to God for his touch and a recognition of my desolation of soul and how much I missed
my husband. Weekly, I was reminded of his loss. We'd
been in the church together many years. He was often in
the worship band. Seeing the band with someone else in
his spot was agony. Hearing songs with particular guitar
sequences which he'd played so brilliantly was like a
knife going in. It was awful. In one sense, when this happened with close Christian friends it was healing and I
could sense the Holy Spirit's ministering touch, but

when this happened in church, where many were strangers, I felt exposed and vulnerable.

I was aware that others were embarrassed and some-times judgemental and sadly, for whatever reason, there were times when I was shunned in these corporate meet-ings, often leaving in tears with no one following to see I was all right. So, I was left in the quandary of needing corporate worship, yet knowing emotions would surface – this made it very difficult to attend in the immediate months and compounded my grief. Instead, I met regu-larly with Christian friends and we worshipped and prayed together and I maintained my personal devotion-al life. In the end, I made the choice that to return to the church where 'we' had both been was no longer an option and I needed to go somewhere where I was 'me' and not part of 'we', where people would accept I was grieving and not have expectations or make demands. Thankfully, I found this in an Anglican church in my local town, where grief and joy could both be expressed.

I certainly learnt from this experience (and sadly every other experience of grief I've had), that the modern church has a long way to go to learn to 'weep with those who weep' (Romans 12:15, AMP) and 'mourn with those who mourn' (Romans 12:15). My heart was lamenting loss – so very evident among people in the Bible and especially in Psalms but I was often confronted with a theology and attitude that only wanted victory over suf-fering: that if you pray hard enough and have enough faith, bad things don't happen to you. Personally, I sus-pect it might be the reversal. Many of the most humble and holy Christians I know or have read about, who exhibit the fragrance of Jesus, have known excruciating suffering. There's little room for the 'dark night' in the contemporary soul and yet church fathers have always talked about this, almost as a rite of passage in the Christian's walk.

Tip: For someone observing a person crying in a church service:

You might wonder what to do. It is usually quite straightforward to identify whether a person's tears are because God has gently touched them with joy, love or acceptance – or if their tears are caused by desolation. The tears themselves will be different and so will the person's visage and body language. Desolation brings anguish – observed through hiding the face, bowing, curling up, self-consciousness, embarrassment or even leaving a service.

If you truly want to help them, please do not ignore this person, thinking you are intruding. There are several approaches you might adopt. Simply sitting next to them and putting a gentle hand on their arm will let them know you are there; offering a tissue and asking if they'd like company. Don't push to try and hug them demonstratively unless you know them very well and don't intrude on their grief or draw others' attention to it by your actions. They're feeling exposed and vulnerable. It is kind to shield them as much as possible from idle curiosity. Gently ask if they'd like you to pray for them. (Don't ask them if they're all right. They clearly aren't.) Think how you're praying. No trite prayers please. Grief is a process and is normal. To short-cut it can be detrimental, so whilst God does bring 'joy after tears' (Psalm 126:5) and 'a garment of praise instead of a spirit of despair' (Isaiah 61:3) don't add condemnation or striving by suggesting a person is wrong to mourn. Yes, the loved one

> *may well be with Jesus in heaven but it is only kind to acknowledge that the person left behind feels a tearing loss in their heart and has to adapt! I'm convinced this awful physical tearing is a result of the Fall. When God first created Adam and Eve in the Garden of Eden, there was no death. However, after they disobeyed him by eating forbidden fruit from the tree of the knowledge of good and evil, the whole human race came under a curse. With this came death (Genesis 2–4). God did not design us for the separation of death, but for eternal living, so is it surprising it hurts so much?*
>
> *Be kind at all times.*

Some of the best help I experienced was from a small group at an Anglican church who prayed for me several times after a service. They just held my hands, prayed silently and cried with me. Their love meant I didn't have to hide the desperation and pain I was feeling. They gave validity to the awfulness of what I was going through, which was terrible. I didn't have to pretend. What a relief! The last thing I needed was Christians who felt I should 'be through it by now', or that I was sinful expressing my loss – it was seen as a lack of faith. So many times I heard 'you're doing so well' or 'so-and-so will be fine – they're strong.' No! We're not strong! None of us! It's God who is strong. It's his strength we need to pull us through, his everlasting arms underneath us, his comfort. Through the tears we cling to him and he wants us to. There is no other formula, despite those who think there is.

I think my favourite verses in the whole Bible are these which refer to Jesus in heaven and how he, personally, will wipe away our tears (Revelation 7:17; see Isaiah 25:8).

See his tenderness and care! He shares our pain and doesn't belittle or diminish our suffering.

Strangely, I also came across a certain strain of competitive grieving. It struck me as very odd, but people who'd been in my situation, or bereaved years before made some odd comments, which hurt immeasurably. Things like 'of course I had to get on with my life. I had children.' The implication being that I was 'wallowing' in grief. Who needs this kind of condemnation? None of us can get inside another's grief and never once did I experience God's disapproval of where I was at. Be kind to one another.

And so tears come in many forms. For me they poured out of a broken heart and came in layers.

When my husband died I grieved for him. However, two of our elderly dogs, both of whom had been rescued by us, were put down the day after he died. It was the right time for them and I'd even talked to Geoff on the phone that day. He'd said we should talk about it when he got home but of course he never returned.

But I had no room to grieve for these two companions. My grieving for them came months later – a much shorter process, but still necessary – as did the finality of my childlessness: nine months after Geoff died I had to have a hysterectomy. It was final! I was just forty and it was the end of 13 years of longing, waiting, hoping, praying and believing in total faith for children. I'd miscarried three times but kept believing my time would come. We'd had many scriptural and prophetic promises over the years – but it didn't happen and I am still a childless mother – a woman with a mother's heart and a mother's love but no children of my own. So I had to acknowledge this grief alongside the grief I felt for Geoff.

Why do I mention this? Just that sometimes one death will bring up grief from a previous one. When my

husband's father died, he started to grieve again for the
mother he lost when he was ten years old and been given
no opportunity to properly mourn at the time.

And as Christians, we may find certain promises we
received from God also die. The future and destiny we
fully believed he was leading us into is obviously not
going to happen. How do we deal with this?

Be warned, there are Christians who will start telling
you that you misinterpreted and they'll imply that you
were wrong. It can't have been God – 'His word never
returns void' (Isaiah 55:11, AMP), 'He doesn't break his
promises' and therefore you misheard or they were false
prophecies.

This is how I faced that issue. Geoff and I had received
many, many prophetic words. They came from all directions: from Christians who didn't know us walking up to
us and saying God had impressed on them that we were
to have children, to being called up at a national confer-
ence, to our elder having a word the very first time we
entered his church, to friends, to friends of friends. Even
before all the words – and many times afterwards – God
had spoken to me individually through the Bible, even
whilst I was still engaged. These same scriptures came up
again and again, often when we were losing hope. And
these words did not refer to children in heaven (i.e. the
ones I'd miscarried). These scriptures referred to children
on earth. Yet – at the end of the day it didn't happen and
I was left with a problem. Was my God cruelly playing
with my deepest longings and emotions? This was not
any kind of God that I related to.

So, I sought God himself. For days, I went before him
in anguish because I believed him to be a God of his word
and if the very foundation and character of the God I had
believed in for over twenty-five years was wrong, then I

no longer had a faith that was based on truth. Becoming a Christian hadn't been straightforward. I'd grappled with issues over a number of years, wanting intellectual answers and even winning a debate that God didn't exist. I finally gave my life over to him at a powerful meeting, where I encountered him personally. I'd known that if I were to follow this route of Christianity, it would be all or nothing for me. So, now, to be faced with the possibility that I'd got it wrong scared me. Either I was deceived, in which case so were all these other mature Christians and respected teachers, or there was something else.

So what happened? As I sought God, I was aware of his acceptance and pleasure at my honesty and even my probing questions and anger. Eventually, having reached a place of 'God I need to know!' which might sound quite demanding, he answered me! He led me to a scripture in a very well known passage, all about the saints of faith – Hebrews 11. Initially, I was so angry. How dare he rub my nose in it! I started reading, thinking he was once more playing with me (and almost thrusting my 'failure' in my face), until I reached the very last verse, which literally leapt off the page at me. 'These were all commended for their faith, yet none of them received what had been promised' (Hebrews 11:39). It brought truth into my situation, diffused all the arrows of unbelief, all the whispering of other Christians about lack of faith and not believing the words and he brought peace. God alone led me to a verse which shows that not everyone receives what was promised. The odd thing was I didn't need any more explanation than this. I needed to know I had heard correctly and that my foundation was intact. I didn't need to know the theology behind why he'd allowed it to happen.

This restored my faith and hope. I could look once again in the faces of the people I knew were pitying me as deceived. I knew I hadn't been and my assurance came directly from God. It also meant I could start trusting him fully once again and believing in his nature, as consistently good.

You may have your own issues you need to take up with him.

Tip: *God loves honesty. He's big enough to handle our doubts, anger and questions. He answers – sometimes specifically, sometimes by taking away the need to know. But he does hear and he does care. He knows our every thought and our every need. Take your questions to him. Don't let any tiny root of bitterness or doubt take hold because again, the enemy wants nothing more than to use this death to knock us off course as Christians. Be encouraged. Be honest.*

Chapter 3

How Can I Help?

> Sometimes I think this is just too awful
> To be happening
> Let alone, it's me walking through it.
> I want to yell out for sympathy
> For hugs
> To be allowed to cry
> Because it's so awful what's happening
> I can barely cope
> I wonder will I cope?
>
> K.S. O'Brien

As we've been going through this book, you'll already have come across *Tips* for helping and in this chapter I'll be expanding further. Again, I'll share from personal experience and offer suggestions.

One thing I've observed, in hindsight, is that the help I needed was like concentric circles. Right at the centre were a handful of very close friends, my mum and her husband. The next circle were still my friends, who knew me well. Then there was a wider group and a fourth circle of people I really didn't know that well.

Each group of people offered different types of support and intimacy.

My mum and her husband, Eddie, had both been widowed and so knew something of what I was going through, as did another friend, Caroline, (these were the people I turned to the night Geoff died; they played a significant role during the first intense months of grief and beyond), whereas my friend Joy, although younger, had already lost her mum to cancer and knew the depths of grief. These four people, plus another couple, formed my inner circle. It was not designed like this, it just happened.

These people were able to give first-hand help because they'd either been there, or were particularly close to Geoff and myself. I didn't have to explain day-by-day where I was at or what was happening. They were involved in the details. As one of them put it, 'We're in for the long haul', long after others disappeared. How right they were!

Between them, they lifted many of the practical tasks off my shoulders. Eddie dealt with my solicitors and the inquest surrounding Geoff's death, being my representative. He then only communicated with me on a 'need to know' basis, sparing me some of the awfulness and tearing apart of Geoff's character which went on in the courtroom as blame for the accident was apportioned, each side trying to prove their party's innocence and the other's guilt through dangerous driving. He took a huge load off me, even when it went back to court, as the other driver appealed his conviction.

He also prepared me for simple issues, like being ready for post arriving that mentioned Geoffrey O'Brien – deceased. I still quiver when I read that, but he forewarned me. In many ways, he stepped in where my dad would have, had he been alive. He even had a 'pep' talk with me about my health and looking after number one, when I was fighting the decision to go ahead with surgery. He was right.

My mum had a different role. She was my anchor, an unchanging focus and the one person who'd known me longest in my ever-changing world. I didn't have to pretend to not be hurting and she was able to give me an 'insider's' view of grief. She could pre-empt some of the struggles I'd face and forewarn me, or put it into perspective. She acknowledged talking to photos of my dad, just as I did Geoff's – neither of us actually talking to them as though they could hear or communicating with the dead – it was just part of letting go. She also shared about the very odd feelings and emotional rollercoaster, where every man who comes across our paths is considered as potential 'husband' material. It was a very strange phenomenon, and until she raised it, I'd thought myself very odd. She said it'd stop at the first anniversary and to the day, it did! I would never have known that was part of grief and would have berated myself, or worse, been tempted to act unwisely. Then she warned me that whilst it's lovely entertaining, watching couples leave your house is really, really hard as you turn to an empty house and prepare for bed, alone. She mentioned that some friends would prove their weight in gold but that others would disappear and they did. Her sharing helped me know that I was walking a path others had trodden before me. It helped enormously.

My two close friends, both of whom had known Geoff, gave me the day-to-day support, whilst another couple, though geographically distant, were amazing in their constant love and communication with me.

The local friends were always on hand. Often they dropped what they were doing and just came. One gave up virtually a year of weekends to drive over to be with me! I was so self-absorbed, it was only afterwards I realised what a sacrifice and commitment she'd made to me, at a considerable cost to herself.

These friends fielded many of the inquiries from others about how I was doing – even months down the line. It was sometimes quite onerous for them and they'd admit they often wanted to shout 'ask her yourself, she's on the phone!' These were the casual inquirers who felt better that they'd asked, but perhaps didn't really want to get too involved. Some were also supporting me prayerfully and I'm grateful that they did.

They were also there when I faced various hurdles. They were the ones I didn't have to explain myself to. I could cry with them and break my heart, express my doubts and know they wouldn't leave me or try to come up with pat answers. They walked that first year with me, as I tried to adapt from being one of two, to being one. I thank and salute them for their friendship and love.

Outside this inner circle were other friends, many close but sometimes separated geographically. These people kept in touch regularly, sent cards reminding me of their love and God's – don't underestimate the power of this expression! They would ring and let me talk about Geoff.

And then there was the wider group. These included work colleagues and other church friends and neighbours. They wanted to help but not intrude and they came into their own practically. At this stage I have to mention how incredibly supportive my teaching colleagues were.

I went back to work within two weeks of Geoff's death. It was really hard, having to convince everyone else that this was right for me. So many voices said I shouldn't and it was exhausting having to justify myself. However, my grief counsellor was superb. She hit the nail on the head by identifying that teaching – my work – was the only thing that hadn't gone into freefall in recent weeks. It was the one unchangeable and as a result provided some stability. Intuitively I'd known this. After all, I was now on my own at home. What was I meant to do? Wallow? Think? No thanks – there was enough time for that anyway.

My colleagues were wonderful. One very perceptive lady (who'd lost her niece) had told the staff not to ask me how I was but to be as normal as possible with me. What sane advice! Yet, I was aware of a multitude of 'little' kindnesses and thoughtful gestures. My Head of Department changed my timetable, relieving me of two very 'difficult' classes. I was given extra free time. Resources and Schemes of Work were sorted out for me, put in place so that I could function with minimum preparation. And there was constant back-up. Any disruptive students could immediately be sent to colleagues' classes and a couple were even transferred altogether. And on the odd occasion when it did get too much for me, an emergency back-up teacher was already allocated to take over my class. I just had to ask. How blessed I was by their support.

As I recall, there were only two particularly dire days. One was during a lesson just three weeks after Geoff's death. An ambulance siren sounded on the road outside school and a Year 8 boy, knowing exactly what he was doing, started laughing and gloating, 'Ha, ha, ha, somebody's dead!' I held it together, just, as I could see the shock on the other students' faces and knew they would deal with him themselves. However, I fell apart later, in the staffroom and was picked up by concerned colleagues, who also put steps in place to prevent it happening again.

The other time, the day of Geoff's inquest, I was suddenly overwhelmed by the enormity of what was happening and couldn't face teaching a Year 11 exam class. It was the morning break and I was still in the staffroom, the bell just having rung to resume lessons. I broke! Within minutes, the blink of an eye, all the senior teaching staff were with me, including the Deputy Head and Pastoral Head. Someone organised to take on my class and I was led to the Pastoral office. To show how absurd I felt, I remember laughing, through my tears as these senior staff peeked around the staffroom door, ensuring no kids were present. Then they swiftly ushered me up the stairs to the privacy of the office. Sweet tea was provided and a safe place to cry. They shielded me, protected me from casual stares and unkind comments from students and cared for me, before releasing me home – and they'd even have ensured someone came with me if I'd wanted it.

These were my wonderful colleagues! Thank you.

The other wider church friends also wanted to help but needed more directing. The Christians often wanted to 'minister' to me, or would ring up to ask 'how are you?' which I always found a dreadfully difficult question. The exhaustion level physically and emotionally was terrible – with police dealings often daily, lawyers, administration of the estate as well as day-to-day living. They didn't realise how terribly hard it was to have to repeat and go over the same things. So often, I was misunderstood. In fact, the help I really needed was in practical daily living. Being back at work and preparing the house sale meant there was so much to do. Even the drains blocked and overflowed at 10 p.m. one night and I ended up having to rod them myself, in the overflowing effluent. Likewise, some rats had decided to take up residence in the roof and despite the 'rat man' saying they'd take themselves off to die, some decided to go belly up in the garage. It was as much as I could do to deal with this on top of everything else.

In the end, a work party from church came and cleaned the house, did some touch-up decorating, so that I could sell up. But even that was hard. I know it sounds ungrateful but this is part of grief. I was reeling from having to leave the house anyway but suddenly my whole house was full of excited people, chatting and laughing, even watching the cricket on TV as they helped; whereas, for me, my world was falling apart. I had to go out into the garden to escape because of the intense pressure of all these happy people. It was a bit of a jaunt for them and they felt useful – and I was grateful, I really was, for the assistance – but I was overwhelmed.

Other memories of special help include my neighbour's children calling to see me, which they often did. They realised I'd been crying and the next thing I knew I was being invited in for an evening meal. It was one of the very few meals I was invited to and I had a proper meal for a change.

So, from these experiences I can draw up a positive list of how to help a grieving person – and provide a 'please don't do this' list too!

Tips: Do

- *Offer practical help.*
- *Invite the person for a meal.*
- *Go round with a meal, suitable to be frozen.*
- *Let them speak of the loved one.*
- *Offer specifically e.g. can I cut your grass, or turn up with a toolbox – what needs doing?*
- *Be thoughtful.*
- *Think before speaking.*
- *Offer to pray.*

- *Do some shopping but don't necesarily expect them to provide a list, so go for staples.*
- *Offer to walk the dog.*
- *Baby-sit the children, so they can go out or sleep.*
- *Think up a little treat at a weekend and invite them. Something as simple as inviting them out for a coffee fills the time.*
- *Believe the best at all times, even if things look like they're going pear shaped. You don't know what's really happening and the pressures they're facing.*
- *Keep offering, ringing, calling – even if you don't get a response. Remember, many do this in the first few weeks and it's overwhelming to have to keep replying. But inevitably, these offers tail off and then you'll be needed. Also, they might just be too tired to respond.*
- *Sit and watch TV or a film together. Provide company.*
- *Remember big occasions e.g. the anniversary of the death and acknowledge.*

Don't

- *Assume the worst or judge people because they are not receiving the help you want to give. Work with them and ask them the way they need help at this time.*
- *Keep questioning all their decisions e.g. when clearing out the clothes it's a very hard and personal time. It does not help if someone then chips in 'are you really ready for this' or 'are you sure it's not too soon?' Reality check – it's never going to be easy but it has to be done! Help don't hinder.*

- Say 'you know where I am if you need me' or 'you know I'm here if you need anything, just ring.' It's really hard to initiate asking for help. It's much easier if you check in regularly and ask specifically 'what about that shopping?'
- Don't expect it to be easy for them to walk into church. It'll be very, very hard. Memories and meeting people are tough. If they skip church, don't condemn but ensure you're there for fellowship, prayer and worship in the home setting.
- Don't keep asking them how they are unless you're prepared for a truthful answer, tears, anger or expressions of depression. Really want to know if you ask this question.
- Don't give platitudes or trite scriptures.
- Don't judge.
- Don't ever offer help or invitations and then not deliver.
- DON'T SAY any of the following – 'You'll soon get over it'; 'You'll probably remarry'; 'I know how you feel'; 'It's early days'.

It's a long list but see how many ways you can assist and avoid adding to pain.

As I began to forge my new life, the parameters of friendships began to change. Some came along with me, others began to drop away. Sadly, as I've already indicated, you may be misunderstood during your grieving and constant forgiveness can become the norm.

I remember being utterly exhausted that first month. Sleep at night was elusive and I resorted to sleeping whenever I could, often during the afternoon. I lived in a big old house, where I couldn't hear the front door bell. I relied on the dogs to alert me someone was knocking. But sometimes they didn't hear either. As a result, some people starting saying I was rebuffing and refusing help. It hurt – deeply.

It was all I could do to hold myself together and to get through a day. I didn't need people criticising me because I wasn't available when they called by. It was often only later I even knew they'd been – when a comment was dropped into conversation – because they'd not left a note. Others genuinely believed that when I put a note on the door to say I was sleeping that I was spurning help. I wasn't, I was sleeping but I would have been perfectly justified if I had needed space. In the first week after Geoff died, I had two hours alone. That's all and as an introvert that was quite overwhelming.

> *Tip: For the person wanting to help:*
> *Please believe the best of people. Even if the grieving person doesn't respond as you'd expect and appears churlish, realise the depth of their pain and forgive. Helping should never be on your terms at this time but motivated by thoughtfulness and kindness.*

One other area I would like to mention is boundaries with other people. A grieving person must put these in place: what is and is not acceptable. This means knowing who you can and cannot trust. Sadly, some people are drawn unconsciously to a grieving person or a tragedy. They seem to want to be a key player in a mini-drama. This can be incredibly dangerous to the grieving person, as that other person is actually draining them and may be emotionally needy themselves. They will drain what little reserves you, the bereaved, have. It will often be disguised as thought-fulness but there is subtle manipulation which you will sense. Be firm, be wise and take charge. You do not have to let everyone into your private grief and space.

Having said this – there may well be a shift in the balance of friendships during the grieving process. Some friends will blossom and show their true worth. Others will not get in touch, maybe ever again. Try to understand. They just don't know how to cope with death and if you do meet someone in the street who crosses over, which does happen, forgive them. I had this happen but found out later that the lady concerned had just lost her own mother in tragic circumstances. She was overloaded. Believe the best of people. Try not to take offence.

Finally, another interesting dynamic is how different people play different roles at different times. My widowed friend who gave me some of the soundest advice – 'you now know you can get through twenty-four hours', after that first day was complete – was very instrumental during the first year. She'd been there and she anticipated my grieving.

After a year, I found I was looking forward and needing to. Three years on there are many new people in my life who never knew Geoff. They've only ever known me as Kathy, not as part of Geoff and Kathy. And that's healthy. I'm rebuilding and you will too.

Chapter 4

What Do I Do With All This Pain?

*D*ead but not forgotten
As I lie awake
Remembering
With aching body
Your every move
And screaming aloud in pain
Despair of unheld hugs
No more words of love
Gone in death
Forever

K.S. O'Brien

I've already talked about the pain you'll experience, both physical and emotional, and there may be times when this will envelop you. It might seem more than you can bear. Is there anything that you can do in this situation? I would suggest there are a number of things and, without any desire to offend, I would caution you not to be too 'super-spiritual'. Whilst God cares very deeply about our suffering, we also need to engage common sense and accept physical help. For instance, if we cut ourselves we apply a plaster. If our teeth hurt we see a dentist. And if our soul is hurting it might be appropriate to see a doctor. I'm the first to admit that I was once in the camp that believed anti-depressants were a sign of failure as a Christian. I've changed my mind and I'll tell you why.

Even before Geoff died, depression had started to creep up on me as our desire for children failed to be realised, year after year. When I presented myself at the doctor with heart pain, he diagnosed depression. I argued fiercely that I wasn't depressed, so he put me through many tests, including an ECG. All came back negative. When he suggested a short course of anti-depressants, I swallowed my pride – because let's face it, that was the main issue – and took them. The physical symptoms stopped.

Then when Geoff died, I was open with my doctor, recognising I'd need all the help I could get to face the future. She suggested I see a grief counsellor and arranged that for me through the surgery. She also prescribed a course of medication. This time the anti-depressants, whilst not taking away any of the emotions of what I was experiencing, did take away the excess pressure which could have pushed me under. They gave me enough breathing space to just about cope. It was part of me choosing to be good to myself and not struggling on unaided.

We all know depression can be caused by a chemical imbalance in the brain, so why do we not accept help? Diabetics do! Those with an under-active thyroid or heart condition do. Is the state of our mental well-being less important, more of a stigma? And even if the depression is triggered by circumstances, so what? Why stigmatise the use of medication and cut ourselves off from a potential lifeline at a time when we really need it? We do not need to make things more difficult for ourselves than they already are. To me, this is practical common sense. I know God is in the business of healing. I've seen and experienced healings first-hand, but not in every situation. We cannot dictate when supernatural intervention will occur and it's not a lack of faith to accept alternative assistance.

I've also come to realise, though I still struggle to come to terms with the fact, that because of circumstances and tragedy, I now have more of a predisposition to depression. I have to be alert to the warning signs and take preventative action. This usually involves something as straightforward as re-evaluating my work/life balance. I make sure I'm not over-committing myself in the work place and with church commitments, at the expense of relaxation and time with friends; the things which re-energise me. When I start to feel isolated I'm in trouble. If I start to feel overloaded, I have to stop. But it's part of my scar – I don't choose to reopen a weak area and must take steps to avoid this. You might find yourself in a similar place too one day.

In this state we have to be rigorous with our thought life, taking every thought 'captive' (2 Corinthians 10:5). I'm not saying it's easy but all too quickly we can fall into a pattern of thinking which leads downwards. Stop and listen to that internal voice sometime. You might be surprised how harsh it is on you. You know the type of thing. 'Nobody really cares about me!' 'They've all forgotten, how could they!' 'And where's God in it all? He doesn't care about me.' STOP and return to a favourite Bible verse. Ignore the unbelieving voice that argues against doing this. Maybe turn to Psalm 23 or Psalm 91. Read aloud. Ignore those doubts. This is truth. Your feelings and thoughts are not truth. God does love you, even if you don't feel it at this moment in time. He is committed to you. He wants, passionately, to be involved in your mourning.

> *Tip:* Catch your negative thoughts. Counteract them with scriptures which define the true nature of God's character. For instance, 'The Sovereign LORD will wipe away the tears from all faces' (Isaiah 25:8), 'Come to me, all you who are weary and burdened, and I will give you rest' (Matthew 11:28), 'Do not be anxious about anything, but in everything, by prayer and petition, with thanksgiving, present your requests to God. And the peace of God, which transcends all understanding, will guard your hearts and your minds in Christ Jesus' (Philippians 4: 6,7).

So, we are taking practical steps to help ourselves. As I mentioned, one of these for me was to accept grief counselling from a qualified professional attached to my GP's surgery.

This truly was a lifeline. I'd never experienced counselling, never imagined needing to and was somewhat humiliated by my needs. I remember being embarrassed initially at my first session, trying to be seen as this 'together person' who really didn't fall apart that easily. How utterly foolish I was! Appearances – as if these really matter! My heart was in shreds. The man I adored most in the whole world, dead in a horrific accident. What was I thinking? My life was in turmoil and I was bothered what this person would 'think of me'. Basically, I was scared of being rejected, of showing weakness because I would seem a 'lesser' person than I 'should' be. Oh, how grief unearths our ugly side! I was shocked at my own duplicity.

Used to being the one ministering pastorally, the one others leant on, I learnt just how hard it is to be on the receiving end. I also learnt how incredibly beneficial it is – if only we weren't so stubborn and proud!

I had six sessions and they were an anchor in the rollercoaster weeks following Geoff's death. Once started, I could barely stop talking and sometimes crying. Together, we worked out a strategy and prioritised what was important and what wasn't. Feelings were given their rightful place and credibility, as was my vulnerability. I bounced issues off this impartial outsider who wasn't emotionally involved in my turmoil. These times were a breath of fresh air and very positive. When I hit a particularly bad low a year or so later, I requested similar help and it was just as effective.

What I'm saying here is not that everyone will need counselling or anti-depressants; far from it. As always, I'm expressing what happened to me. However, I wanted to alert you – be prepared to consider options for help, even if they 'stick in the throat' because it's a route you never envisaged having to take.

You might also like to consider some creative expression to release the pain and acknowledge it to yourself. I created an abstract embroidered textile. Blue centrally symbolised the flow of my marriage, backed on a black open weave silk fabric. A red explosion right in the centre was my broken heart, which bled away down to the bottom right corner. I often felt as though my heart was literally bleeding, the pain was so intense. Then, for months I came to a standstill, until one day I picked the textile up again. I could now add coloured strands of gold and yellows, reaching upwards rather like sunrays. They expressed some of the new hope I was beginning to feel and which was beginning to emerge. Now, complete, I look at my work and it expresses two years of my grieving process in a story which is personal to me.

Tip: Here are some possible creative outlets for your emotional pain:

- *Writing a diary, for your eyes only.*
- *Composing music.*
- *Writing poetry.*
- *Drawing or painting a picture.*
- *Sculpture.*
- *Writing a song.*

During this period where you are really hurting, you might want to operate a 'damage limitation' policy. You're probably walking close to the edge emotionally. To take on another person's troubles or pain might be too much. For those who are naturally empathetic and kind, it can go against our nature to withdraw our support from someone else – however temporarily. Our own struggles can make us want to reach out to someone in pain even more – but I would caution you to hold back. A time will come when your own grief will have lessened and then you will be a tower of strength to these people – but not just yet. For now you might have to let someone else be the one who helps. You may not be as available as you have been because you will be guarding your own heart as it heals and this is very necessary to come through grief whole.

Tip: You might well find others are drawn to you because of your bereavement. They're desperate to tell someone of their own heartache and think you'll understand. But be warned – especially in the early stages of grief, it's unlikely you'll have the resilience

> *to take on another's pain as well as your own. Just because they come to you does not mean you have to respond. Gently guide them elsewhere for their support.*

I still get people telling me the most dreadful tragedies, often of people they don't even know. It's quite bizarre. They think I have a personal monopoly on understanding tragedy, whereas in fact I have a lesser resistance than most to hear about these things. I'm sensitive by nature and have learnt to cut across someone now and ask them to stop. Like bees to the honey pot, people enjoy chewing over juicy details. I've learnt to say 'please could we change the subject' or 'let's pray for those involved, shall we?' This jogs people back to reality but in a kind way. People forget you are still living through the aftermath of death and, unless they've been there, they're unlikely to realise the impact it can have on you.

> *Tip: Seek out those people who energise you, whose company you really enjoy and avoid those who drain you, or just want to dump their problems and have you sort them out.*

Remember, this is survival mode, doing what will get you through this particular period as whole as possible and hopefully having grown in maturity. There is a way through and what we've been talking about here – honesty with yourself – is a crucial part of the process; realising your own limitations. Pretending to others or yourself doesn't help anyone in the longer term.

When a day seems particularly dire and the pain unbearable, it's good to cope with it in chunks. Rather than waking in the morning to face a whole day, think only in terms of the time up until morning coffee at 11 a.m. Don't berate yourself if you're existing hour by hour. I remember a brief period where it seemed I was functioning minute by minute. It seems odd, looking back, as I can barely remember it now but I know it happened. I had to live in the moment because to look beyond it was so bleak I would flounder. It's been a valuable lesson, as I do now tend to live each day at a time and not get too hung up about the future as much.

Thinking of that one piece of advice given to me by a colleague who'd experienced her husband being killed in a road traffic accident was 'be kind to yourself'. It struck me as a bit odd at the time but I've come to value that phrase so much. It's more profound than I'd realised.

So 'being kind to yourself' often meant letting myself rest if I was exhausted, even if the grass needed cutting or a meal cooking. It meant allowing myself to indulge in little treats – a new top, some scent, a short trip away. It gave me permission to do things I really enjoyed. So in all the struggles, learn to face the pain, raw though it is, acknowledge it and find a coping strategy that works for you.

> **Tip:** *If you can't sleep, or find it hard to rest because your mind is full, try listening to music you like, or a story tape. This can capture your mind and help you rest, even if you don't sleep. Be careful what type of music: only what brings you peace, not sadness.*

Chapter 5

Why Me?

*S*ometimes it's so dreadful I can barely contain it
The physical pain of missing you sits
Heavy on my chest
I barely want to breathe
The tears are so near
But these tears never end and bring no healing
They just go on and on and on
Until I can cry no more
But just ache
With desperation
Trying to come to terms with it!

K.S. O'Brien

People have often assumed that I would ask, 'Why has this happened to me, God?', whereas in actual fact it's not a question that's arisen. My questions have generally been along the lines of 'How do I cope with this?' It doesn't mean there haven't been deep and searching questions; there have!

Some of the questions I had to ask. I needed answers. Coming from a theological background that believes in spiritual warfare I needed to know, 'Did God take Geoff home or was he taken out by the enemy?' who I know comes to 'steal and kill and destroy' (John 10:10). I've already mentioned my crisis of faith over the unfulfilled prophecies but there were other ways in which my faith manifested and the depth of my faith shone through.

I was amazed by the closeness of God, especially in the very early days. Right from the moment I knew Geoff had been killed on that Tuesday evening, Christians in my church were praying. My pastor lived close by and he immediately rang the pastoral co-ordinators, who were able to inform house group leaders. As house groups met on Tuesday evenings, prayer was activated virtually instantly. Gradually the grapevine spread further afield and Christians across the country were praying for me. I'm still amazed how many people were covering me in prayer during that time and that is why I'm not totally surprised by the intense intimacy I experienced with God.

There were times when he came to me physically. I clearly remember standing in the kitchen of our home alone at about the time Geoff would have been due home from work. I was bereft and gasping for breath because of the crushing pain. It was at that moment I sensed God walk towards me and wrap me in his arms. I was physically held. Comfort came, as well as tears. Several other times, I've felt him come up behind me and hug me.

It was a significant event for me, as Geoff and I had a daily ritual on his return from work. I'd be in the kitchen preparing tea and would stop, so that we could hug. Not a quick hug but one that lingered for a few minutes and then we'd get on with the rest of the evening. But for both of us these hugs reconnected us after a day apart and were a deep expression of our love and need of each other. Oh how I've missed those hugs! But God knew the little details and that evening he greeted me with a hug!

Another time, he spoke to me so clearly I'm still not sure if it was actually audible, but it was an answer to a very specific question I had.

Then there were the visions; several of them. All of them included Geoff and some included our three children with him. Each time I knew I was looking through a portal into a different spiritual realm, a glimpse directly into heaven. Forgive me if I don't share the details. These were so precious and intimate to me that I hold them closely to my heart and cherish them. They were given to me privately to comfort me and I choose to keep them that way.

However, I will say this. These visions were not my imagination and they changed my whole spiritual outlook and assurance of eternity.

They ran like videos whether my eyes were open or closed and with them came the sense of God's closeness. I can't imagine that. Comfort, joy and love were the result and an intense knowledge of the reality of heaven. I became aware of how thin the veil really is between this world and the next and also what a dim reflection this world is compared to the glory of heaven and what I saw. Everything here seemed dimmer and more sullied; though I can still appreciate an amazing sunset, I'm aware the earth is 'groaning' (Romans 8:22) as it winds down to its ultimate end. It is merely a preparation for what lies beyond. Heaven really is home.

Heaven is a subject we may never truly think about until someone close to us is dying or has died. We can have a rather fuzzy idea of what it's all about, often muddled in with images of angels, clouds and singing. The Bible talks about our 'heavenly dwelling' – a very real place, somewhere that once Christians die, our spirits live 'away from the body and at home with the Lord' (see 2 Corinthians 5:1–10) – which is so good that the apostle Paul could say: 'I desire to depart and be with Christ, which is better by far' (Philippians 1:23).

And what a future Christians have got to look forward to! The Bible says that this earth will pass away and be replaced by a new earth and a new heaven. God will wipe 'every tear from [our] eyes. There will be no more death or mourning or crying or pain, for the old order of things has passed away' (Revelation 21:4). Some things will be different! It's clear that marriage as we know it won't exist (Matthew 22:30). But we've got a home prepared for us for ever by Jesus Christ (John 14:1–3), and we know the way – through Jesus himself: the way and the truth and the life (John 14:6). We will spend eternity worshipping and loving Jesus.

We know that death is therefore only a temporary separation and we will be reunited with people we love who have died. In Matthew 22:32, Jesus said that God was not the God of the dead but of the living! How wonderful and what hope this brings for the Christian.

Another truly wonderful experience happened when I was at a particularly low ebb. It was the middle of the night. I was on my own and I was missing Geoff intensely. There was no one to turn to as they were all asleep in their own homes and I lay in bed crying. I don't even remember if I was praying, sometimes it was just too hard. But, someone had been praying for me because I became aware of an angel in my room. Softly an angel wing lowered over me. I could feel the softness of each individual feather and I could hear the words of Psalm 91 in my mind 'under his wings you will find refuge' (v 4) and then I slept peacefully.

Likewise, nine months later as I woke at 2 a.m. in a hospital bed having had a hysterectomy – feeling so much pain physically and emotionally – I was lying on my side unable to move when suddenly the most beautiful smell wafted by my nose. It was a bouquet of freesias, a heady sweet smell, yet there were no flowers in the room. It was the fragrance of the Lord and it brought courage (Song of Songs 1:3).

These are just a few of the intimate moments but the reality of God's physical touch brought so much comfort. I don't experience it very often now but what a testimony to the power of prayer.

> **Tip:** *Pray specifically for the bereaved to experience God's love and expect him to show up, just as he promises to.*

Having these spiritual experiences reinforces the head and heart knowledge that God truly does care. This is vital if we are to cope with the onslaught of doubts and fears which surround a death.

Remember, seek God for yourself for answers to your questions. One of the answers I received concerning Geoff's death came on a card from his sister. 'The righteous perish, and no-one ponders it in his heart; devout men are taken away and no-one understands that the righteous are taken away to be spared from evil. Those who walk uprightly enter into peace; they find rest as they lie in death' (Isaiah 57:1,2). It brought comfort and some resolution to my questions.

And sometimes there's a choice involved. 'God, I thought you loved me!' It can feel the exact opposite. But God is working all things out for his good purposes.

Choose to believe it. His plans are to 'prosper you and not to harm you, to give you hope and a future' (Jeremiah 29:11). Whatever foul thing has happened, he wants to bring good out of it.

Tip: Write out some personal scriptures, ones that minister to you. Post them somewhere you'll see them frequently or carry them with you. Have them to refer to as a reminder.

We can be so desperate for answers we'll do anything to get them. Be wise and be careful. One of the greatest deceptions there is, is to believe the dead loved one wants to speak to you again. Especially if there wasn't a chance to say 'goodbye' or 'I love you' or 'thank you'. There can be a desperate yearning for one last chance. Resist it! Spiritualist churches, mediums, anything where communication with the dead is encouraged is merely going to compound hopelessness, as well as being strictly forbidden for everyone, in the Bible. (See Leviticus 19:31.) It is deception. Instead, deal with the unresolved issues. Face them.

'But I didn't get a chance to say goodbye.' I didn't either and the very last evening we had together I was in bed by 5 p.m. with a gruelling migraine. My last memory of Geoff alive is of him putting an icepack on my head. Oh regrets! Deal with them.

Tips: Unresolved issues? An argument? You want to say 'sorry' or 'goodbye'. Well do it anyway.

- *Write a letter expressing what you need to.*

- *Hold a private service in your home.*
- *Light a candle symbolising the issue.*
- *Pray and commit it to God.*
- *Float a lit candle out to sea or down a river.*
- *But above all, LET IT GO!*

During these times of questioning keep seeking answers from the Bible too. You'll find your theology possibly changing. Things you accepted or hadn't thought too deeply about will become important issues. You might start to notice that the whole gospel isn't being presented in your particular church, but is slightly slanted in one direction.

I found myself drawn to the laments in the Bible and wondering where the modern expression is today. I found myself wondering why there are so few laments about the state of the world, the tragedy of lives being lived out around us, the suffering there is, the desolation of a world turned away from God. Who is mourning?

I sought comfort in the Psalms and traditional hymns, knowing others had suffered but held firm to Jesus. I clung to the belief that, like Job, good would come out of being so sorely tested. I now know bad things do happen to good people, without explanation. God doesn't play by our rules or confine his ultimate purposes to our little box-like thinking of him.

I clung more and more to the first two commandments. 'Love God and love your neighbour.' Much of church 'stuff' felt superficially peripheral to the centrality of my faith and relationship with God and, to be honest, it still does. Yet my love for Jesus has grown immeasurably, as has the assurance of his love for me. I know now I can't earn his love. I can't be a super-spiritual Christian. I can't do anything except run to him and cling hard, asking him to be sovereign and central in it all. What hope! What security! And yet, despite all of this there are times I still forget this, turn away, and wonder why I feel so lost – until I turn back. But, I'm quicker at running back to him now!

You might have come from a church background that emphasises that if you are a mature Christian then everything is straightforward, tragedy doesn't touch you if you put on the full armour of God each morning (see Ephesians 6:11) and death doesn't hurt, especially if the person's a Christian and has gone to heaven. The reality has shocked you. Death hurts – terribly. I merely urge, please don't go into denial but be willing to let God change and expand your theology, be willing to grow in your faith and understanding. Be willing to allow the Holy Spirit to highlight scriptures in a new way, pertinent to your situation – and be expectant.

> **Tip:** *Have a look at the Psalms and the emotions David expresses. Re-read Job.*

And if you find yourself asking, 'Why me?' I merely reply, 'Why not you?' Since the Fall, suffering has come to humanity. Death is a consequence and is here to stay until all things have passed away. Sadly, though it might still be preached, Christians are not exempt. BUT we do have God with us through the dark valley of Psalm 23 and that's the difference.

> **Tip:** *If you don't hear any answer from God to some of your questions, a time will come when you have to sur-*

render and offer the question to him, leave it there and accept it's in your best interests if he hasn't explained it. Draw a line under the issue and try not to revisit it. In this extreme situation, you'll really have to trust God that he knows best. Remember, a child playing with fire does not understand why a parent snatches them swiftly away without explanation. It's for the child's welfare.

Chapter 6

The Ugly Face

Angry? Am I angry?
'They' say I'm not bitter
that I've coped 'so well'.
But am I angry?

I don't know.

In my mind I have peace about your passing
From life into new life
In my questioning I've heard
Answers that satisfy, that explain, that matter
But am I angry?
At the very core of my being
In my primordial instinct

I have rage
Deep uncontrolled, red-hot
And spewing
Spitting in attack from my very heart of life
At the injustice . . . At the pain
At the senseless waste . . . And Yes
My heart, in pain IS angry
For the YOU I have lost

Will never be again
I am angry that our times
Cemented by love
So often traumatised by suffering
Should end so abruptly
I'm angry that dreams
Promises we held
Never happened
Never will!
Instead fall, dead to the ground
And rot . . . Yet . . . Yet
In anger, is there hope?
That my pain came from
Loving . . . Risking
Stretching into the unknown.
And in my angry pain, as I writhe in the fire's
heat
I can but hope, that One loves me more
So much in fact
That He knew best and
Took you.

K.S. O'Brien

I expect the title of this chapter makes you wonder whatever's next and, for me, it's probably one of the hardest chapters to write. There were times during my periods of grief where I seemed to metamorphose into a monster, spitting and spewing uncontrollably.

To understand the shock of this, I consider myself a fairly even person temperamentally. I'm enthusiastic and lively, passionate, kind and considerate. Only very occasionally do I lose my temper and these times are so rare I can vividly remember each incident. They usually involved those closest to me, my family.

However, during the aftermath of Geoff's death an unexpected rage built up inside. This was terrible to acknowledge to myself and proved quite dangerous. It bypassed my rational mind. That part of me was coming to terms with issues but this rage went much deeper to some primordial instinct at the heart of my being. And there it simmered, red-hot, ready to spew out its volcanic lava with a force that really frightened me.

On one occasion I went off, literally like a pressure cooker exploding and the truly awful thing is that it was at a total stranger. Let me explain and share my shame in a hope that if this rage happens to you, you'll find a much kinder and safer venting place.

A friend and I had been walking my two remaining dogs in a fairly unknown spot, deliberately away from other people. They'd been particularly jittery and unsettled by events. I didn't want to accidentally run into something that would cause them to defend me.

We'd had a lovely walk, as it's a particularly beautiful spot along a river, and were returning to the car. However, we failed to notice another car had pulled up and the owner had a dog. They were hidden from our view by a hedgerow – but not from the dogs! They ran ahead barking loudly. I'm the first to admit that as large dogs, it can be scary having them approach barking. I don't knowingly let this happen.

Having called the dogs back and leashed them, the lady started having a go at me verbally. 'People like you shouldn't be allowed to own dogs! They should be put down.' And so she continued ranting, until I interrupted. By now I was seeing red. She had pushed every button. She'd highlighted the dogs were out of control, which they were momentarily, and I knew it! What if she made a formal complaint against me? She accused me of not being a fit owner which compounded my sense of things being out of control. But above all she implied they should be put down, which was my deepest fear – that I would lose the last thing I had left that I loved – the dogs. I'd already had my family halved overnight with Geoff's death and the older two dogs (the parents of the remaining two). What was there stopping me losing these younger ones too? These were the fears which fuelled my outburst. Rage fuelled by fear.

Before I knew what was happening I retaliated verbally, in a way I'd never normally dream of speaking to anyone. I remember shrieking 'my husband's just died' desperately wanting her to understand my plight – yet feeling this intense anger towards her. Once I started, though, I couldn't stop. It was horrible. Words tumbled out, one after the other. I've no idea what else I said except this poor woman didn't deserve this. She seemed rooted to the spot. It even enraged me further that she wouldn't retreat and put her dog back in the car, so we could pass. She just stood there, taking the barrage until much, much later she did retreat.

I didn't swear but she did receive my undiluted fear, frustration and anger. It must have been truly unpleasant and I've never had the chance to apologise. That is the ugly face of grief. It's very, very ugly.

As a Christian I was mortified – that I'd hurt someone, been so ghastly and so out of control. It took me quite a while before I could forgive myself. Why? Well, it was more than just the above. It was because I felt so much better afterwards. I felt clean, released. A pressure, a weight had gone.

So what would I advise to avoid this? Well, know that anger can also be a significant part of grief and try to channel its release away from people. Don't aim it personally at anyone. There may be very valid reasons why you are angry. I had to work through this with regard to the driver of the car which killed Geoff. There was never any acknowledgement from him, of how his actions had totally changed my life for ever. However, what I chose to do with that anger was my responsibility. Would I let it fester and cause resentment for the rest of my life? Or would I forgive him and move on? I struggled, especially when the inquest was drawn out and I won't pretend it was easy. It wasn't! But I did get to the point where I could let it go and forgive. I'm glad I did, as I rarely think of him and I'm no longer consumed by anger. (See Prayers, Chapter 12.)

> *Tip: Find outlets for anger which won't hurt people. For example: punching a pillow or punch bag; yelling at God; beating the ground with a strong stick. Go for a long run or do something very active which can release the anger safely. Above all, be forewarned and be forearmed.*

After this outburst, I didn't like myself much. This wasn't the 'me' I knew. It was uncomfortable. I was thoroughly ashamed in front of my friend and in front of God. As mentioned, I've never been able to apologise to the lady, so the only thing I could do was resort to prayer. I prayed for her, for God to touch her heart, to diffuse the pain I'd caused and to surround her with his love.

I repented and sought forgiveness from God and from my friend. And then I had to forgive myself but this was much harder. I held on to my wretchedness long after God had forgiven me. I felt I deserved this penance! I was misguided. Whilst not negating what had happened, again pride prevented me forgiving myself. I do so more readily now. It's one of the lessons I'm still learning.

My life was in the crucible and I could feel the heat, as God stoked the fire. You know the chemistry – to purify gold you have to heat it to an intense heat in order for impurities to surface and be removed. I think grief can do this too, if we're willing to work with the master Goldsmith rather than against him.

I learnt from that awful outburst about my humanity and frailty. I learnt that when the pressure's on there are very ugly emotions in my heart and horrid thoughts in my mind. I learnt that whilst I do exhibit fruits of the Spirit – gentleness, self-control, kindness etc. – I'm nowhere near as mature as I had thought I was. I learnt the shocking nature of the ugliness of my own heart. For 'out of men's hearts come . . . evil thoughts . . . malice . . . and folly' (Mark 7:21,22). I learnt literally, that but for the grace of God that's me. I hope a greater self-knowledge has emerged.

However, this is all part of how God turns what was meant for evil into good. Do we turn to him or from him when we fail so spectacularly? Do we rush to ask forgiveness or turn away and nurse our hurt pride? Do we pretend it never happened or do we keep short accounts? So, holding onto God when the heat is on is a vitally important part of the grieving process. We need to maintain open communication through our prayer walk with him. We need to ensure honesty and truthfulness, even when we fail. He does know, after all, so who are we kidding?

You might think 'I'd never do that! How awful.' I do warn you that grief can create emotions you've never experienced before and take you totally unawares. I trust you will seek to release the pressure slowly and safely, rather than go off in a big bang!

The pain erupted
Spewing grief in anguished cries
That penetrated to the centre of my soul,
Piercing the flesh with its darts of fire.
How could this be?
How can it have happened?
Torn in one instant from life
Into eternity
In a cataclysm of metal
Screams . . .

K.S. O'Brien

Chapter 7

Help! I Need a Way Through This!

Your face
To keep me going
Feed my dreams
Keep company to my lonely nights
Alone
Thinking
Too much thinking
In the solitude of my head
As I turn my face into the pillow
Knowing I must blot you from my thoughts
I must
I must
I must
Or despair.

K.S. O'Brien

Having identified some of the difficult issues you're facing, in this chapter there will be some very practical examples of support you can get. There are simple signposts that if followed can keep you focused and direct you through the maze of grief.

Firstly, don't despise support networks. Subconsciously, I think I rejected the idea of plugging into one. I wish I hadn't. I made it harder for myself than I needed to. There's a multitude of self-help groups set up to support bereaved people. These are usually run by people with direct personal experience. Access to this information and groups can be hard. Your funeral director may leave an information sheet with contact numbers. I managed to bury mine under the paperwork involved in Geoff's death. I didn't come across it until a few years later when clearing out the file. I wish I'd accessed these groups sooner. I've enclosed an appendix with some details. If nothing else you'll link with people who know you need to talk and cry. Some might offer an individual contact person for ongoing support, who might even visit.

> **Tip:** *If you want to attend a meeting but are finding the thought of a roomful of strangers too daunting, consider asking a friend to take you the first time.*

For instance, I came across a well-established group, Widowed and Young, two years after Geoff died. It's a national organisation with local groups who meet socially. I wish I'd known sooner. By the time I did, I was in a transition period, no longer sure if I wanted to be identified as a widow by relating to other bereaved people. I was trying to put it behind me. I thought I was ready to do this but it was somewhat premature. If I'd already had established friendships within the group I might not have rushed to try to move on too early.

Church-wise, there are some churches that do have established bereavement ministry teams. People on these teams are dedicated and remain a point of contact with the church. Visits are regular, if not frequent, throughout the first and into the second year. They can be a lifeline for someone finding church too painful and continue to make that person feel part of a church community. This eases the transition back into attending church services when ready.

Tip: If your church doesn't have a bereavement team, it might be worth considering setting one up. I would suggest some guidelines for people invited onto the team.

- *Be a good listener.*
- *Able to keep confidences and not gossip.*
- *Compassionate and kind.*
- *Empathetic.*
- *Able to commit to long-term involvement.*
- *A mature Christian.*
- *A deep desire to serve – I don't pretend it's an easy option.*

At times of crisis families often really pull together. We find ourselves calling on them for deep support. I did. My immediate reaction when the policeman arrived was to ring my mum. I didn't need to ask, I knew she would be there for me, even though geographically we live over one hundred miles apart. She and her husband, Eddie, dropped everything and just came, even though it's a two and a half hour drive (arriving in the early hours the morning after Geoff died). I was so grateful and they stayed for two weeks. No warning. Everything put aside to help me.

If you've family living close by, this support can continue down the months.

However, I do want to mention something here, especially to Christians where there is such an emphasis on the family. We live in a very fragmented society. The very word 'family' no longer means the nuclear family of parents and children. We have step-families, single parent units, and many people consider they no longer have a close family member. The assumption that family rallies around when there's a death can be a myth. Often split geographically, it can be impossible. So many people have to move to relocate for study or jobs. So when a death occurs they literally cannot be there to help.

What a great opportunity for friends, especially Christian friends, to step in. I have friends who became as close as brothers and sisters to me. So, if you are a friend, please don't back out because family turn up in the short-term. You might be the very person your friend needs right now.

For a start, friends provide stability if family is separated by distance. They might well know the bereaved person more intimately than a family member does. They also know the locality and infrastructure – where the shops and doctors are. They know the friendship circle, who will be supportive and who is best discouraged from being involved. A good friend is invaluable.

There are some very odd notions surrounding friendship, as if you shouldn't share the depths of life because friends walk away whereas family stick by. Rubbish! That view is outdated, outmoded and frankly harmful. It can leave someone from a small family, bereft. I stress it strongly but simply because Christians who are in large families – often with generations of Christians – really can be blind to the needs of the modern society. Often, they are so used to having a parent, sibling, grandparent or nephew on hand, that they have not needed to develop this depth of friendship.

> **Tip:** *Christians be aware. Notice whether the bereaved has close family but never assume that your friendship is an intrusion at this time. Pray – especially if there are no Christians in the family. They need that prayer support, which larger Christian families are privileged to experience in an ongoing way.*

So the place of friends is central to recovery, as is fam-ily if you're blessed enough to have a good relationship.

One surprising support network I discovered was via the Internet. Late at night, when I couldn't sleep I often experienced my darkest hours. It felt like the whole world was blissfully unaware of my nightmare existence. On several occasions I resorted to emails. It all happened quite unexpectedly.

I'd been searching for a particular book on Christian web-sites, when I entered a site for a particular mission. There was a newsflash asking for prayer. A young husband's wife had just been killed in a road traffic accident. He was left behind with their adopted daughters. My heart broke for them. I was a year into my mourning and just that little bit further down the road. So I emailed him, to offer my support, saying if he ever needed to contact me in the middle of the night just to email me. As he was in the USA I'd more than likely be awake. And that's how it started. Our friendship grew and we did email consistently for a while. When he came to remarry a lovely lady, I was even invited to their wedding.

I now have three or four regular email friends abroad. We often pray for each other, send off urgent requests and are just honest about where we're at. What a surprising source of support. There are several Christian sites where people chat and want to build friendships online. (I have included some information in Appendix.)

Now, I said there would be practical tips in this chapter on getting through 'those days'. We all have to face them when someone dies – hurdles which we'd rather not have to jump – places, people, anniversaries. I came to refer to them as skittles.

Very early on, after my mother had returned home, some of my closest friends came to stay with me for a while. The four of us faced things together. (Recognise some friends will also be grieving for the deceased.)

On one particular day we decided to knock down several skittles. A skittle represented something very difficult which had to be faced.

We started the day by going to scatter Geoff's ashes. This meant visiting a place particularly special for us both. We'd been walking there for over ten years, often two or three times a week. It's a high scarp ridge, in the area of outstanding natural beauty where we lived – called the Blackdown Hills, in Somerset. From this spot, on a clear day we'd look down onto the whole length of the Culm Valley, up to the Quantock Hills in the east, Exmoor, across to Dartmoor and down the valley to the sea at Exmouth. It felt like the whole of the SW peninsula was spread out at our feet. It was the obvious place to scatter his ashes.

We held our own informal service, each praying and thanking God for Geoff's life and for knowing him. There were many tears as we finally let the breeze take his ashes. This was a major skittle knocked down.

(What I didn't notice at the time, only subsequently, was I'd placed his ashes in the centre of a ring of young sapling oak trees. Over the years they've continued growing and will make a memorial grove in time that only I'll recognise. I'd considered planting a tree at the crash site but was worried it might die. Instead God provided this solution.)

We then faced skittle 2 – driving up to see our old home, the first we'd owned and only left a year and a half previously.

Then on to skittle 3. We visited the crash site together. I'd not felt brave enough until then but with these friends I could face it, traumatic though it was. There was still debris on the road, several weeks later. However, it helped. I'd been having flashbacks of his accident, even though I wasn't present. I'd find myself seeing him being thrown through the air and smacking onto the ground. These had plagued me. It helped to see the actual site and gradually these flashbacks did stop.

As Geoff had been killed on his way home from work (an hour's drive from home) we drove by his office, skittle 4, and then on to Exmoor. He worked all over Exmoor, a dream opportunity and one he loved. However, Exmoor was 'our' place. We spent as much time as we could there and had a special haunt where we'd always spent our wedding anniversary.

I didn't want to lose Exmoor as well as Geoff but I knew it meant visiting early on. So skittle 5, visiting medieval Dunster where we'd spent our tenth anniversary and on to skittle 6, Porlock Weir and our favourite pub. Thankfully, our preferred seat by the fire was occupied and we had a drink in a different room. Probably just as well. It was hard.

Skittle 7 was driving back across the moor that he loved so much, past Dunkery Beacon and back along the River Exe to home.

Even now when I see a glimpse of the moor in its autumnal splendour I remember our times together. Happy, happy days.

There was, however, one special place we didn't go that day – Watersmeet. It's interesting that I've not been able to return yet. It's still too painful, whereas I've revisited all the other places. I suspect it's connected with not having faced it early on; it's almost become too big now. I wish I'd knocked that skittle down in the early days too.

So, that's an example of what I mean by skittles – facing a difficult event or time or place.

> **Tip:** *You might want to buy yourself a miniature skittle set. I did and at the end of a day I'd knock my skittles down – to show to myself how brave I'd been and to acknowledge a positive step forward had been taken.*

Of course, there were other 'big' skittles that loomed large. As Geoff died in May, I had a summer holiday looming, then our wedding anniversary in September, Christmas, my fortieth in February, the hysterectomy in March and the first anniversary in May, plus his birthday.

This was what I did to cope positively. I was proactive. I made some decisions early on. I wanted to go on embracing life as fully as possible despite the pain. Your way and approach will be personal to you.

Regarding the summer holidays, my friend Joy and I decided to go to Scotland to a fisherman's cottage where Geoff and I had been once before. However, it didn't hold many memories of him as he'd had food poisoning and spent the week in bed. What I remembered was lovely walks with the dog along the bay, looking across Loch Fyne and following the river by the cottage. It would be an easy place to return to rather than sad and, as we both love Scotland and I could take the dogs, it was ideal.

I won't pretend it wasn't strange travelling with a friend and not Geoff. I realised how we'd loved travelling together. Time in the car was quality time where we talked in depth.

During the holiday we both continued our grieving (Geoff was one of her close friends, so she was also grieving his death) and this involved some symbolic acts. There was a particularly poignant time one dusk. The river ran next to our cottage and out into the loch. We held a time of thanksgiving for Geoff's life and what he'd meant to us. There were many tears. We then lit a floating candle each and put them out into the river's flow, watching them until they flickered out. Mine was extinguished much sooner than I wanted it to be.

However, during that holiday God was very close and spoke to us often in ways only we would recognise. For me, it was through wildlife. God's always blessed me with exciting glimpses of secret wildlife because it brings me immense pleasure. I distinctly remember on the rainy morning, being driven to the crematorium, looking out of the window and seeing three herons. To me, they were a private message from God, saying he was involved and watching over me. He knew I'd appreciate seeing them and they've always seemed an appropriate choice for a death. Beautifully striking birds but grey – not flash like the kingfisher or woodpecker I'd usually long to see.

Ever since then God has been sending me herons at key moments, as continual encouragement. Even at times flying right over my house, when I had a hard decision to make. A few months ago, I looked out of my study window across to the field and three little egrets (part of the heron family) were perched in a tree. They're very rare inland in the UK and I was so thrilled. They were pure white; it was a special blessing.

Likewise, Joy gets rainbows. She'll even ask God for them specifically if she's needing encouragement. We saw rainbows galore on that holiday, including a white translucent one rising awesomely out of the sea. Spectacular!

> **Tip:** *Be aware that God wants to remind you personally of his love in a way you'll understand and that will bless you. Be on the lookout.*

Another skittle was our wedding anniversary. We'd always made a big thing of it, more than birthdays, but I decided to no longer recognise the day. My vows of marriage were until 'death parts us' and I was no longer married. This was my way of coping. Instead, I now concentrate on celebrating Joy's birthday, which happens to be the day before and deflects my associations.

Then Christmas, what a hot potato! I'd already been struggling with family Christmases because it highlighted being childless. I know Geoff and I had been misunderstood by deciding to stay at home but the alternative was to be cut raw by an issue we were struggling with day in, day out. It wasn't helped by the fact that my sister-in-law and I had held a conversation one year where we both admitted this was the year we'd be starting our families. Only it happened for her and my brother, but not for us. Whilst delighted for them, every time I celebrate my niece's birthday it's a reminder that my children never materialised. I've had to minimise damage and have tried really hard to get through this issue, not always successfully. More often than not though I've been awkward and misunderstood. However, I didn't want to blight other people's Christmas with my issues.

And now, I had the additional loss of Geoff. What in the world could I do to tackle this head on?

In the event, this skittle, once knocked down, became my happiest Christmas ever – apart from Geoff's absence.

Joy and I went off to Prague. (You may be thinking how blessed I am to have a single friend willing to holiday with me but Geoff and I had always had numerous friends, including single friends, within our marriage.) That trip to Prague was blissful. It combined everything I could have needed in terms of being kind to myself: a fascinating city to explore, beautiful sites, cultures, midnight mass in a packed cathedral and a touch of luxury. It was a good decision. The following year we went to Salzburg and walked the snowy hills of *The Sound of Music*.

Then it was my fortieth birthday. Yikes! Geoff had been killed 12 days after his. I tried not to think about that too much.

Whereas we'd not really celebrated birthdays that much, I decided to have a party for close friends and go overboard. Using my creativity again in a therapeutic way, I held a middle-eastern soiree. Decking the lounge out with sari materials, I created a Bedouin-style tent, cooked a load of middle-eastern food and invited my friends. It was great fun preparing and sharing the evening.

Then came the anniversary of his death. Again I decided to be proactive. May was going to be tough. Starting with Geoff's birthday, it also contained the date we were engaged, his death and funeral dates. A lot to take in.

On the actual anniversary of his death, I took that advice again of being kind to myself and booked into a health farm. It was something I'd never done before. Some serious pampering and I loved it! I laughed as I floated around in the flotation tank, slept during the massage and relaxed in the beautiful surroundings. It was a good move and a major skittle was faced – that first anniversary was behind me!

> *Tip: Think about how you want to deal with big skittles. There are no 'oughts' or 'shoulds'. Go with what's right for you. Just as I wore raspberry red to the funeral, be yourself. It's your expression and don't worry what anyone else thinks. You are the one trying to get through this process whole. You might even want to write yourself a letter or card reminding yourself how brave you're being. I even posted one to myself. It really helped.*

So, let yourself have some fun. One thing I really enjoyed initially was a sense of liberation. I no longer had to compromise my decisions and I rediscovered the more adventurous and creative side of my personality. It started to blossom.

One way this was expressed was the creation of my Dream Book. Knowing that with Geoff's death much of my future died too, I started to create a book of new dreams. This contains anything that caught my eye and gave me a flash of desire to continue living – photos from magazines of mountains and Arabic souks, seascapes and city landscapes – places I want to visit. It contains poignant prose extracts and emotional poetry, scriptures that speak to my situation, as well as radiant colours. I packed it full, trying to identify some essence of who I was now becoming, alone but still with a future and destiny ahead. It was amazingly cathartic.

Likewise, when I entered hospital for my hysterectomy, I created a Hope Book. As the situation felt so desperately hopeless, I needed something to hold on to. In it were special words from friends, some of the cards Geoff had sent me that reminded me I was once very much loved, inspirational sayings, cartoons which made me laugh. It was an eclectic mix. Anything that would give me hope was included. I'm not pretending it dealt with all the pain but it certainly helped.

> *Tip: Consider creating your own hope or dream book, or maybe a memory box containing special items. You can then revisit these at your choice of time. Somehow capture the tiny memories which make you smile. For instance, I've listed some of Geoff's mannerisms and favourite things. It's my memory jogger and includes some particular memories. (I'm so glad I wrote them down because my memory isn't one for details and I do forget specifics.)*
>
> *A thankfulness book or memory box can also be a place where you record anything you are thankful to God for: things surrounding the dead person; kindnesses from people since. It's a good thing to have something to refer to especially on days when the last thing you feel is thankful.*

And one final tip – when getting rid of their belongings don't be afraid of change. You don't want to end up living in a museum stuck in your grief!

I chose to move photos of Geoff away. Instead I created a large montage of my favourite photos and hung it on the stairs. It was a place where I could choose to walk on by, or sit on the stairs and linger. However, it meant I was in the lounge relaxing without being constantly confronted by his absence through a photo.

I also had to change routine. That evening hug was sorely missed, so I started eating at a different time and going for a walk when he'd been due home. It helped break the association and ease the ache.

Regarding possessions, be wise here about what you choose to keep. I couldn't understand why I didn't want to hang two particular pictures Geoff had bought me, in my new house. Then a friend asked the pertinent question, 'How do they make you feel?' I immediately replied, 'Sad.' I put them in the garage until I was finally ready to let them go. I didn't want anything in my new home that made me sad. I had a different picture he'd bought me that made me immensely happy. I've stuck with that one!

Remember, you do not have to keep anything out of sentimentality or obligation. You can choose to say 'goodbye'. In the end it's just stuff. We carry the really important things with us anyway, in our memories. You want to emerge healthy and whole and sometimes that involves letting go of a whole host of things. And if family members don't want you to, that's their concern, not necessarily yours. You're the one who has to move on, recreating new boundaries and discovering who you are in this new phase in your life. Be brave and choose wisely, rather than being swept along in the momentum of grief without any control over your choices.

Chapter 8

Watching the Suffering

When a death happens it can be devastating, not only for those closely involved but also for friends and other family members. They, too, can be profoundly impacted by the loss. Even if they aren't, watching the anguish of people they care about can be heart-rending.

Hopefully, in this chapter, I'll offer a few pointers which might help. What can you do when you feel so overwhelmingly helpless? Well, actually, there are a number of things! As you know, I've already put Tips in this book at relevant points. I hope you find them useful. Here, I will try to expand on what is really a very difficult area and one where there are no absolutes. Individual situations vary so greatly.

But, before we get on to that, let's look at you and how you're feeling. You may be experiencing some of the following, in the face of your friend or family member's grief:

- Panic.
- Out of your depth.
- That you want to take control.
- You wish they'd pull themselves together.

- Irritation.
- Inadequacy.
- Overwhelmed.
- That you want to run away and hide.
- You don't know what to say.
- Embarrassed.
- Can't cope.
- Anger.
- Guilt.
- Confusion.
- Desperate to make things better.
- Confused by what you believe.
- Sadness.
- Utterly helpless.

Yes, these emotions and many others assault people in this situation and I would suggest it's normal. Personally, I've not come across many people who are actually comfortable around death and grief. Naturally, we don't want to be reminded of death, nor do we cope very well with another's pain. Primarily, we want to stop the hurting and the desperate thing about grief is that we can't stop the pain. Little we say or do will ease the agony; which doesn't mean we shouldn't try!

So, now that you realise your experience is normal, you have a choice. Do you give in to your fear and discomfort or do you push through it and come alongside the bereaved? The choice is yours.

Firstly, acknowledge that the loved one is in pain. They may be behaving out of character, be irrational or demanding, even unresponsive to you. If you can, try to give them space emotionally to go through this painful time. They may well be inconsolable or seem to be rejecting you. Their grief may appear out of all proportion to what you thought they felt about the dead person. Grief's like that! It can cut through to real emotions and bypass the mind, sometimes unexpectedly.

This is a time which might really test your own maturity of character and faith. There are some things to consider here. Death has a way of making and breaking relationships. How you respond at this time will impact on how you relate in the future. If you stay away because of your own sense of inadequacy, sadly, it may cause an irrevocable distance which will be hard to cross in the future.

I'm not wanting to be melodramatic but to point out that grief changes people. The bereaved person's perception and values will often alter. Things that were previously important can pale into insignificance and new priorities rise up. If you are not alongside, experiencing this shift, you won't be aware it's happening. To then try and catch up some time down the line might well cause confusion and misunderstanding – feelings of 'where were you when I really needed you?'

Temporarily, even a close relationship with the bereaved might also change. Your emotional 'needs' might not be met. Usual pleasantries or thoughtfulness may disappear altogether. So, how should you respond? Well, I would suggest the following:

- Be patient.
- Be kind.
- Don't remember your grievances, forget them.
- Forgive.
- Love.
- Be tolerant.
- Don't be envious of how absorbed they are by the dead person.

- Be polite, even if you're being pushed to the limit.
- Don't be resentful, moody or touchy yourself.
- Believe the best of the person.
- Be hopeful.

Recognise this? Well, 1 Corinthians 13 is a good guide to love, isn't it!

However close you are to someone who is grieving, you are nevertheless on the outside looking in. You may be very intuitive and empathetic but you still won't be able to experience the gamut of emotions which they are going through. The death will push up any unresolved issues in that relationship, as well as guilt, sadness, confusion, anguish, and so it goes on. As a result, you will need to take your lead from the bereaved person themselves.

Different temperaments and personalities will respond in different ways to grief. Some will want to keep themselves busy, others may be totally immobilised. One thing I would caution against, though, is trying to take control – certainly not without consulting the grieving person.

It's amazing how tempted people are to do this and to give endless advice! 'You really should . . . eat, sleep, clear out the clothes, get some fresh air, speak to so-and-so, put that photo away' and so it goes on.

Please – try not to give endless advice! It is very wearying having to counteract it and it's often conflicting from different people anyway. It's an unnecessary pressure and unhelpful.

Likewise, questioning decisions that are being made is equally galling. 'Are you sure you should be getting rid of their clothes? It's such early days.' This question evoked two very strong responses in me. Firstly, I nearly punched the living daylights out of the person – who wasn't even a friend and had not experienced losing someone this close and, secondly, I nearly spat out, 'Well he's never coming back, so it's not like he'll be needing them!' It was really, really tough for some busybody to question this decision. It'd taken me a huge amount of courage to clear out his wardrobe. It was traumatic. The last thing I needed was to have someone question my decision.

Having said this, if you are a close friend or family member and you genuinely believe the bereaved person is making an unwise decision, you might want to carefully double-check with them. This way you're giving them the chance to express doubts or to invite you into the decision-making process, without taking control.

I still remember endless people questioning me about selling the house. I put it on the market a few weeks after Geoff died. Yes, it was very soon wasn't it! But no one seemed aware of the financial implications of his death. There was no way I could keep the mortgage going on the one salary.

So, what can you do? Go the extra mile in thoughtfulness and don't inflict your expectations onto someone else. What help you offer will depend a lot on your personality, commitment and available time. I urge you to be realistic. It helps no one if you overstretch yourself and then have to suddenly withdraw because you are overloaded. Think before you act, especially if you are naturally kind-hearted and emotionally led.

Be Practical

Practical help cannot be underestimated. People who don't want to take on the emotional role – you can really help with your skills here. However independent someone is, there is always a way of easing the load, sensitively. Taking over isn't the solution, nor imposing your approach. If at all possible, take the lead from the bereaved. Depending on what needs they express, possible areas to offer help include the following (some may be repeated from *Tips* in other sections):

- Meal preparation.
- Shopping for general stocks.
- Shopping for tea, coffee, biscuits and milk for all the visitors.
- Providing a hot meal.
- Household laundry.
- Cleaning.
- Ironing.
- Administrative help – writing to banks; photocopying death certificates; notifying endless service providers, such as electricity, gas, local council, passport office, DVLA etc. that there has been a death.
- Phoning people about the death.
- Registering the death at the registry office.
- Contacting funeral directors and arranging a visit.
- Collecting medical prescriptions.
- School runs.
- Childminding.
- Sometimes just being in the house and providing company, especially if someone's too nervous initially to sleep in an empty house. Stay in a spare bedroom, or camp on the lounge floor.
- Providing a lift to church and going in with them.
- Sorting through belongings.
- Taking away clothes to charity shops and recycling other items.
- Car maintenance.
- Help with preparing a house for sale where necessary, e.g. decorating, thorough cleaning, repairs.

- Household repairs.
- Computer housekeeping e.g. deleting 'favourites' files or pertinent personal emails.
- Money advice (if you are an appropriate financially savvy person).
- Offering a financial loan (accounts can suddenly be frozen and access to cash stopped).

Of course this list could go on forever and you will identify many, many other practical ways of helping.

Then, as well as the practical support, there is the emotional side. Earlier in this book I've mentioned how different people fall into different circles of emotional closeness, with only a very few people in the inner circle, but many in the outer circles are able to offer additional support.

Right in the central circle will be people very close to the bereaved. They will walk through the experience with them and the bereaved will be able to be real with these people, without any pretence. These are the people who listen, cry, love and console. They are in the thick of it, step by step. Often they are close family members and very close friends.

If you are not one of these people, please don't impose yourself, however well meaning you are. It really doesn't help for people outside the close circle to keep asking 'How are you?' or 'How are you feeling?' Hard though it is to understand, your sympathy is adding additional unnecessary pressure. Put yourself in the situation for a moment. So much is happening internally during grief. It's too exhausting to try to find words to answer a superficial inquiry. You're on an emotional rollercoaster of stomach-churning proportion. It's only really the inner circle who can ask this question. They are coming fully informed to the situation.

Now, already I know some of you will be affronted and possibly offended by what I've just said. Please don't be! This isn't about you at this time. It's about them – the grieving person. Please just recognise that in grief, people need to feel safe, and they will naturally choose those people they feel safest with, for themselves. If you don't happen to be one of them, look for other ways to offer your support.

Inner Circle

If you are one of the two or three closest people, much of the emotional load falls on you and it can be a very difficult situation to handle.

Despite the urge to make things better, a gently, gently approach is more appropriate. It's natural for the dead person to be praised endlessly. Sometimes, how they are spoken about barely resembles the real person you remember. In kindness, resist bursting the bubble of illusion.

One of the loveliest and kindest expressions of support is – simply listening. Listening to the endless reminiscences, the memories, the details; listening to the same stories, the same accounts, the person who's dead being eulogised, often as though they were a saint – and saying nothing to contradict that impression, because the balance will return. In time the dead person will be taken off their pedestal. You won't need to do it. But to be listened to fully, with 100 per cent attention, is a rare gift. Yes, there may be tears. Yes there may be times you feel very uncomfortable but if you can give this gift of attentive listening, it will be so greatly appreciated. It's also a gift which can be given at any time, down the months and years which follow on.

Don't be tempted to rush it by imposing the practical. The time of talking will end only too quickly. Grant them the dignity of remembering, as it allows them to come to terms more fully with the death. It also cements memories. You may well cry with them, as their pain touches your own grief over this death. Hugging and crying is very natural and comforting. Don't be reserved because of fear. Human touch is a great source of comfort, just be sensitive and take your lead from them.

Your own need for patience and grace will be sorely stretched. You may find it necessary to have someone yourself to lean on during this time, as you minister to the grieving. It can be exhausting. After all, this will usually be on top of your usual routine and daily commitments. This is truly sacrificial giving of yourself because of love. Don't doubt this, it's not easy for anyone.

You might also have to lay aside your own feelings about the bereaved person. You may not have been that enamoured by them or you may be shocked that a relationship you thought was solid is showing up flaws. Death strips away the veneer, people come out from behind masks and the real essence of relationships and feelings is revealed. Sometimes it's truly beautiful, sometimes it's ugly. Try to support, despite your own emotional conflicts – these can be resolved outside of the immediate situation. When appropriate and big issues are revealed, maybe unresolved guilt, recognise that the bereaved person will need a professional's help – maybe their GP or a grief counsellor.

Other Friendships

Whilst only a few are privy to this inner grief, this certainly doesn't mean other friendships are not required, as

I've already indicated. Far from it! Friends and family support will be even more important as time goes on. These relationships can be vital for beginning to build a new life, especially during the few months after the death.

Friendships can provide comfort, a sense of belonging, hope and enjoyment. Social events can push aside loneliness. Friends play a huge part. Do invite the bereaved over for a meal or to join you if you go out somewhere. Something as simple as a trip to the cinema or a garden centre can fill a lonely evening.

You may enter someone's life after their loved one has died. It brings deep joy to still be asked about them. I find Geoff has made me who I am to a large degree and whilst many new friends have only known me as a widow, someone recently asked me to tell them about Geoff. It gave me such pleasure, especially as I talk about him naturally in conversation but so many people ignore it totally. I think there's nothing healthier than acknowledging he was a big part of my life and to bring those happy memories along with me. Chances to talk about the person who's died diminish very swiftly. It's not long before the majority of people will stop talking about the dead person and be embarrassed if you do.

The important thing to remember is to maintain respect and not impose your ideas or agenda onto the other person. Also, that the bereaved person might not always turn to you for support, but may turn to another person sometimes.

This can be rather tricky to interpret but the best explanation is that different people help in different ways. A bereaved person might look to a particular person for emotional support, for the safety to cry, to unburden themselves. However, they might not go to the same person once they want to start socialising again. One person might offer practical help; another, the chance to laugh and forget the sorrow for a night. I would suggest that no one person, not even a spouse, can offer 100 per cent support but that a more healthy way is to see a number of people involved at different levels in different ways.

So, don't be offended if your friend decides to go somewhere or do something without including you – even if in the early months they seemed to rely on you a lot. When you give to them in their grief, it's without strings attached, there's no demand for payment in kind at a later date. You give. Unconditionally.

Relationships and friendships themselves change during the grieving process. An intimacy that grows as a result of death pushing down normal reserve may return to a less intimate level a few months down the line. It's normal and, although challenging for those involved, can lead to the continuation of healthy, whole relationships. Most bereaved people are in time able to move on but problems come when they can't, or don't want to. And this, sadly, is where some people do seem to get 'stuck' in grief – unable to come through to accepting their current life and rebuilding towards a future. Sadly, their identity is linked backwards to the person who has died. This can be unhealthy and where someone may need further grief counselling, perhaps years after a death has occurred.

For those who are elderly this might be particularly applicable. The burden which then falls on family and friends is hard and the bereaved person might quite clearly not want to move on. Their whole life, maybe a marriage of many decades, is behind them. How can we help? How can they help themselves?

I would suggest sharing the load and calling on experienced helpers, to assist the person who is grieving.

Cruse (see details at the end of the book) is a bereavement organisation which offers many extended services for times such as this. Similarly, Help the Aged also has support systems available. Trained grief counsellors and bereavement visitors, people other than the immediate family/friends, can alleviate the burden by being willing to visit, befriend and listen to the endless reminisces.

Older people don't have to feel as though their lives are over, even though the readjustment can be particularly difficult. Opening their eyes to being able to see that they have a unique place in guiding those younger than themselves might bring a new focus to their remaining years.

Tips: *Some ways to help people move forward include:*

- *Finding new places to visit which hold no memories.*
- *Changing set routines e.g. mealtimes, regular visit times.*
- *Eating something you love but didn't used to cook.*
- *Finding new TV programmes, perhaps comedies, which you didn't watch together.*
- *Starting a new hobby or interest or sport with no associations.*
- *Making use of the time you've freed up to do something just for you.*
- *Slightly altering the living room layout.*

Grief counselling might make this clearer for them.

Some things I did were: discover a new comedy on TV – *Frasier* – which replaced watching ones Geoff and I had watched together. I started doing mashed potato because he loathed it but I loved it. A friend and I discovered a delightful pub on the canal which was totally new to me, so didn't make me sad. I took up some textile art to occupy myself creatively of an evening and joined a group to learn more techniques, which resulted in meeting new friends. I also explored different music and bought some which I know Geoff would not have enjoyed but I did.

The wholesome process of grief allows for a time when you want to move forward and leave the sadness behind. In fact, the intense sadness lessens and you realise happy memories no longer bring tears too.

Thoughtfulness is the key. What can you do to personally express your support? Individually creative responses are called for. Here are some of the things I remember people from my wider circle doing. They really blessed me!

- Some of my students bought me a bright purple flowering plant.
- One student made me a tiny bright yellow clay duck 'to cheer me up'– I still keep it close by.
- Other students made a large card. On one side was a picture they'd drawn of the accident (which was tiny) with a large illustration of heaven with rainbows and colour and beauty. (These children were not Christians.) The whole class had signed the back with greetings.
- My home group helped clean and decorate the house prior to selling it.
- Help with sorting through belongings.
- Disposing of belongings.
- Administrative support with paperwork.
- Dealing with Geoff's computer files.

- A friend coming and just sitting quietly alongside me, saying little as other visitors came and went.
- Someone providing endless teas and coffees to visitors.
- Taking the lead in conversation.
- Shielding me from casual visitors and unwanted inquiries.
- Answering the phone.
- Providing shielding at church from over-solicitous people who barely knew me.
- Help with shopping.
- Company at weekends.
- Representing me at the inquest, so I didn't have to attend.
- Months down the line, asking if there was any help I needed.
- Regular checking in with me, every few weeks.

> *Tip: Please remember to ask if help is needed rather than expect a bereaved person to contact you! For some people, it's just too hard to do that.*

- Cards, showing you care.
- Letters reminding me I was loved.
- One minister's wife, who heard I was bereaved but didn't know me directly, wrote regularly. She expressed kindness and thoughtfulness, with chitchat and loving concern. She still writes a couple of times a year. What a blessing. What kindness. She still realises that I miss Geoff, three years on.
- Cards on important days.
- A Valentine's card – one from a friend, one from a friend sending it on behalf of Jesus.

- Many acts of kindness and thoughtfulness.
- Flowers for no reason (Geoff used to buy me flowers often, just as an expression of love).
- Planning social events and taking the initiative.
- Finding new places to explore with no memories.

These are things I can easily and swiftly remember but they were all initiated by other people. Knowing that I was being prayed for was also vital to my wellbeing.

Remember, one person can never supply all the needs. If you find yourself being pushed into this situation pull back. Take stock. Realistically assess what you can and cannot do. Keep those boundaries in place for your own well-being and to assist the grieving person. Small gestures are as welcome as large ones.

Helping a grieving person, as I've mentioned, can be very sacrificial and demanding but don't do it at the expense of your own health, either physically or mentally.

We all know love believes the best at all times, doesn't remember wrongs and covers a multitude of sins (1 Corinthians 13; 1 Peter 4:8). Whilst they are grieving you may see a different side of their normal character. It might not be pleasant but love bears all, forgives, is kind and long-suffering. Not a popular message but the fruit will be wholeness of the person struggling to come to terms with death.

So, resist the urge to hurry the grieving person. We live in a society that gives no recognition to grief. It expects people to take a few days' compassionate leave and return already 'over it'. The reality is that grieving is a process and that takes a number of years. Few people make allowances for this. Please be one of them, so that three years on from the death you are the one to mention their name. You are then the one to share a happy memory because you are someone who hasn't forgotten that to the bereaved this person is still alive in their memories. They are as much a part of them as when they died. More often than not they don't want to totally forget them.

So, in conclusion, I would stress: believe the best at all times. Allow for irrational and maybe out-of-character behaviour. Go the extra mile in tolerance, offer practical support and above all be willing to listen attentively and with kindness.

Chapter 9

How to Find Peace

They've forgotten now, most of them
The shock of your death
The trauma of the news
The terrible, huge changes
The end of life as I knew it
And your name is barely mentioned
One short year and you've passed into oblivion
Except for the very few
Yet even they scarcely seem to feel your loss

Yet 'I', 'I' plunge into the abyss
Of unexpected wretchedness
As wave after wave of grief hits me
As fresh as the moment I first knew
As physical as gut wrenching as
Those first revolting days
Of creeping flesh and cold sweats
As my body succumbed to shock
In an effort a useless, useful effort
To keep me surviving
For what?
For this – an emptiness of broken dreams
And forgotten promises

When all I know is that
He we love most above each other
Took us at our words
And accepted our lives of sacrifice
On the altar of burning
Your flesh was consumed
The ultimate offering
Mine cast adrift
To seek once more my love
And ask 'What shall I ask?'
No words – I collapse, prostrate
Aware, only of my need
For loving everlasting arms to hold me
Close to the eternal beating heart
For life is but a shadow
Of all that is to come!

K.S. O'Brien

Questions But No Answers

One thing I can guarantee as you grapple with the issue of death, is that at some point it will bring questions to the surface – probably immediately if it's a sudden or tragic death, or maybe after a few months. Death is now a reality. You are facing it. It happens – to all of us.

Even as Christians, we find ourselves re-evaluating what we really believe. Personally, before Geoff died, I had a certainty that life continues beyond death, that there is an everlasting eternity. As a young Christian I'd read and re-read passages about heaven and the end times. I believed it. I still do.

So when Geoff died, I knew he would be with Jesus. That wasn't an issue. He believed and professed Jesus as his Lord. He was saved. Like me, Geoff had made a conscious decision to hand his life over to Jesus when he was a teenager. We both believed that 'God so loved the world that he gave his one and only Son, that whoever believes in him shall not perish but have eternal life. For God did not send his Son into the world to condemn the world, but to save the world through him' (John 3:16,17). Jesus himself said, 'I am the resurrection and the life. He who believes in me will live, even though he dies; and whoever lives and believes in me will never die' (John 11:25,26). It is clear that this offer is there for everyone, the gift of eternal life. We don't deserve it through any goodness of our own but through Jesus dying on the cross in our place, taking our sins away and creating the relationship with God forever. (If you've never made the decision to hand your life over to Jesus and would like to, turn to the prayer in Chapter 12.)

I knew that Geoff had made this decision for Christ and so when I read what Jesus says in John 6:40: 'My Father's will is that everyone who looks to the Son and believes in him shall have eternal life, and I will raise him up at the last day', I am reassured that Geoff is in heaven.

But what about people we love who die and as far we know they don't profess a faith?

I want to be honest here. I believe the Bible's account of eternity, either in fellowship with God or eternally separated. To consider someone I love being separated is the closest thing I can imagine to hell. I'm not going into the theological issues regarding hell here! What I do want to do is flag up the emotional fallout for Christians when a non-Christian friend or family member dies. How can we begin to resolve such issues? How can we deal with any guilt we might feel? How can we cope with never, ever seeing them again? For after all, isn't the reuniting in heaven the thing which brings

Christians such hope in the face of death? For us, it's a temporary separation.

I have a number of thoughts on these issues. Where once (before I experienced multiple deaths) I was very black and white in my beliefs, now I'm far less sure; I'm more aware of the existence of God's overwhelming love for everyone, believer and non believer alike. I'm awed by his mercy, whilst still aware of his justice. And I'm overwhelmed by his mystery. His ways are so infinitely different from anything I can comprehend. I only get a glimmer of understanding. So, ultimately, when I've found myself in this situation, I've reached a place of total honesty with him.

When I have lost a friend who wasn't a Christian so far as I knew, I've confessed my anxiety, my confusion, my fear concerning this person's eternal welfare. If necessary I've confessed my negligence in not communicating his love adequately – with an eye to not repeating that lack in the future. I've then had to release my concern for that person back to God and leave it there. Ultimately, it's his role, not mine. I don't believe in praying for the dead. I do believe our chance is whilst someone is still living. So, I leave the grief and burden with God. And if I'm tempted to return to it, I remind myself that God is in charge not me.

It really isn't easy. I'm not pretending that. We love them but the comfort is that God's love is infinitely greater. I hope that doesn't sound clichéd but the reality is that his love doesn't want even one to perish without knowing him. He and he alone looks into the heart and knows the truth. So, a line has to be drawn and we walk away from the issue. It's one we cannot resolve this side of the grave and to try to will only lead to misery.

Tip: *Prayer concerning someone's eternal destiny:*

Dear Lord,
I come to you today because I'm hurting. (Insert name of the person who has died) has died and I'm troubled. I don't know where they stood with you and it's eating me up. I'm anxious. I'm confused. I'm scared.

I do say that you are a good God, who is merciful and just, who knows the end from the beginning and who sees into the heart of every person. You alone know everything. I know you died for (person who has died) and for me. Therefore, I now commit my concerns for (person who has died) to your goodness and ask that you will take this burden from me forever.

Please comfort me with the knowledge that your ways are best for everyone concerned.
In Jesus' name I ask. Amen.

The same goes for other questions which will be thrown up. Sudden, tragic and cruel deaths can be traumatising for those left behind. Even if the dead person's a Christian, the way they suffered can be crippling to our faith in a God of mercy, love and kindness.

How do we come to terms with a God who allows this? How can he care and look on and do nothing?

I've even wondered if God was preparing me for Geoff's death. In the months leading up to the accident, we'd spend loads of 'time out', primarily as Geoff was finding it hard heading towards forty and re-evaluating his life. We spent hours and hours walking, talking and spending time together; really special memories now.

I also had an article published in *Bella* magazine, about the way God brought us together as a couple through a dream I'd had. It was even entitled 'The Man of My Dreams'. It was published in the April before he died and afterwards it felt like I'd written his tribute.

These are the 'biggies' surrounding our faith, questions which have been debated ever since Jesus was walking the earth. Suffering happened then and it still does today. Why doesn't God intervene and stop it? Why does he miraculously heal some and not others?

I've grappled with these issues over the years. I'm not going to pretend to provide answers. I can't – sorry. Instead, I'll suggest ways through the questions to peace.

Firstly, there's a need to acknowledge the doubts are there. Acknowledge them directly to God. If you are angry, incensed, even hate him (oh yes, love can turn to hate when faced with this), be brutally honest with yourself and with God. One of the saddest things I come across is Christians who pretend it doesn't hurt and that they don't have to grieve. That somehow they get divine exemption to bypass the process. There is even teaching which suggests we should only celebrate because the dead person is now in heaven. Of course we celebrate this fact (and it is the Christian's hope, as I have mentioned before) but I feel very angry at the denial of what the bereaved person is facing.

Do you feel your genuine grief is being denied? Do you feel condemned because you are grieving instead of rejoicing? Please, do not deny any grief you are feeling. Death entered with the Fall. We were not designed to cope with it. Any death creates a tearing and the need for readjustment. If nothing else, we just plain miss them, don't we! God knows this and he longs to comfort you. Please let him.

Be very careful not to slip into the desire of seeking comfort from anything but the Truth. Unlike much New

Age teaching, their spirit doesn't remain behind with you. Sadly, they are not just in the next room and any 'presence' you feel is not them. Comfort comes from God's Holy Spirit. Ask him to speak to you.

So, I earnestly encourage you to talk to God openly and truthfully throughout. Don't hide behind religious language or how you think you 'should' behave with him. Be real. I have included a prayer in Chapter 12 that might help. It is important to release your confusion and anger over the death of someone who's suffered or died tragically. Be honest – if necessary, brutally so. There have been times where I've shouted at God, 'How could you do this to me – take everyone I love and leave me behind!' I've been angry and tearful. There have been other times when I've questioned how he could let Geoff die so young with no obvious fulfilment of his lifelong dreams. There have been many times when I've so wanted to be a mother of living children that the physical pain has ached like a gaping hole inside me and I've had to gasp out my prayer to him – the questions, the anger, the rebellion, the self-pity. 'How could you do this to me?'

And no, instant relief didn't always come but something did and does happen. In my situation, he's graciously answered some of my prayers directly with literal replies. But he has also left many questions unanswered. Instead, they've been replaced with a sense of no longer needing to know. The intensity and urgency have been lifted and I've also watched the changes on my own character and value system. It's as if I've been watching someone else's life as an observer. Gradually, I'm seeing glimmers of gold emerge from the crucible. Maybe only tiny specks but dross is being burnt up.

Other times he takes me right back to earnest prayers I've made in the past. 'Use me to impact the lives of others', 'Make my life a testimony to you', 'Use me God', 'Break me', 'Change me' – prayers made faithfully and in genuine commitment. I almost hear him whisper, 'I took you at your word and this is what was necessary.' I couldn't foresee the outworking or the necessary refining needed in my life to bring about God's ultimate purposes and bring me to a place where he could actually use me more effectively. Sometimes, for short periods, I've regretted those prayers – but not any more.

When I was given a Bible verse from the Amplified Bible (at the start of my missionary training, a long time before I was teaching) it never occurred to me that it would become my life verse. 'Have I not commanded you? Be strong, vigorous and very courageous. Be not afraid, neither be dismayed, for the Lord your God is with you wherever you go' (Joshua 1:9, AMP). Throughout the years God has taken me back to it, again and again. When I first received it I suspect my main response was one of pride. Now, I run, fast sometimes because I know to fall into the hands of the living God is often painful before I see the good results.

So, do you have unresolved questions? Doubts that are crippling you, that you're ashamed of? Questions which threaten to rob you of your faith? Anger at the appalling hand you've been dealt? Face it, head on. Deal with the gremlins. Don't give the enemy a foothold. Talk to God openly and honestly, calling on him to help you through this. If you choose to harness up with him at this time of loss you will grow. I can guarantee this 100 per cent. He will bring comfort and he will restore hope. It won't be at our bidding. It won't be to our agenda or in our time-frame but his everlasting arms will be underneath and he promises to be with us wherever we go. The truth is nothing can separate us from God's love through Jesus (see Romans 8:39).

We have a choice. Once you've been to God – and this might be on many occasions over a considerable period of time – and you may still have no answers, at this point LET GO. Admit to yourself that you will not know and draw a line, once and for all, under the situation. Commit to yourself not to return to it but to hand it over completely to God – acknowledging his wisdom is complete and his character is good. Yes, it's a step of faith and with that choice, let it go.

If you don't, chances are that it will eat away at you, bringing disquiet and doubts – whereas God promises peace and rest. 'Do not be anxious about anything, but in everything by prayer and petition, with thanksgiving, present your requests to God. And the peace of God, which transcends all understanding, will guard your hearts and your minds in Christ Jesus' (Philippians 4:6,7). This only comes when we are honest and willing to trust him – despite the pain, despite the hurt, despite the doubt, despite everything. Trust isn't a feeling, it's a choice. It's where we get our will in line and choose to believe the goodness of the character of God. Peace does follow, as do comfort and rest for the soul.

Spend time reading Psalms. Feed your soul on Psalms which speak to you and comfort you. Spending time in this way, with others who have suffered and walked the bleak path, allows you to see how they dealt with it by drawing on God's comfort and allowing his Spirit to minister directly to them, body, mind, soul and spirit.

So, despite every inclination, choose to turn to him and don't run from him.

Tip: *Here are some Psalms to start you off:*

Psalm 6
Psalm 13
Psalm 20
Psalm 23
Psalm 42
Psalm 63

Chapter 10

Christians Are Human Too!

To say 'I love you' encompasses
Yet YOU
Fill my mind
Continually
Constantly
Your ever-present presence
Consciously
Unconsciously
On my inner screen
Your face flits
In all its moods
Expressions
Played
Replayed
Until each word uttered
Is repeated
Onto my consciousness imprinted
Gone, gone, gone
But here.

I took so much for granted
The way you talked to me

And shared your childhood memories
The here, then, that's how it used to be

And now, can I remember?
How quickly I forget or
Maybe only half listened
To what you hadn't told me yet

Your stories, often told
So easily dismissed
Oh, how I wish you could repeat them
I've wished and wished and wished

It wasn't too late to listen
To listen and not dismiss
To listen with full attention
So I'd remember every little bit!

K.S. O'Brien

This is the chapter which may well prove the most difficult for me to write, because I will be talking a bit about
the 'dirty laundry' of church life. I'll be honest about the
times when Christians let you down. As this book is being
written to try to minimise the effect of fallout after a death
and to stall regrets, I want to prepare you in advance for
some surprising reactions you may encounter from
Christians. I hope I'll also be able to offer a way of navi-
gating the storm, if it comes your way.

Prior to a death, Christians may well have been uniting
in prayer for healing. Some will be certain God is going to
heal, so when the person dies they're confused and feel
let down. It may be the situation you also find yourself in.
Don't be surprised if people look to you, the bereaved, for
answers and some kind of explanation. They might

expect you to have some special insight into the situation – which, in all honesty, is unlikely. So, as well as your own emotions, you are now faced with coping with others' crises of faith.

My suggestion is to be open. Share your gratefulness for the prayer support and express your hope it'll continue but unless you have total clarity, try not to get embroiled in another's doubts at this time. Your own emotional reserves will be needed 100 per cent and there are others who can come alongside them. You are not responsible for how they feel.

You may also find yourself in the unenviable position of implied blame. It's seldom expressed to your face but to other Christians and it goes something like this – 'of course, there must have been hidden sin that left them unprotected' or 'unbelief was a stronghold, they weren't in faith for healing' or 'of course this sort of thing only happens if they've disobeyed God or not been praying for his covering. The enemy can't touch you if you're in the right place with God.'

The implication through these comments and thoughts, is that we or the dead person should have *done* something more; that somehow we were lacking in some area and the death was self-inflicted. Get the formula right and suffering is not part of the Christian's life walk. And it's true – the Bible does indicate that long life is a blessing from the Lord (Psalm 91:16).

However, how can any of us really know! We also believe God is sovereign over our lives and over death. The kind of judgement mentioned above is of no help whatsoever to a bereaved person. It's appallingly hurtful. The time for raising any such issues is during life, not after death. No one can know categorically, despite the assertions made in some denominations.

So, if you find yourself the unwelcome recipient of such judgements, or sense others are speaking unkindly about the situation, what should be your response? Firstly – forgive them instantly and keep forgiving every time it arises in your mind. Secondly – don't dwell on it, as it will compound your hurt. Thirdly – remember 'there is now no condemnation for those who are in Christ Jesus' (Romans 8:1). This is the truth. Talk to God about it – then give it no more attention! You've more important things to expend your energy on than to wonder why people are behaving in this way.

> ***Tip:*** *To those of you who are on the outside of the grief – please resist the urge to criticise or judge. You really don't have the full understanding of the ways of God and it's more important to love than to be right. Remember, you've not been in exactly this situation and it's unlikely you know how hard it is.*

What about the expectations you might have of your church fellowship when your loved one dies? I'm not sure we even realise beforehand that we have these expectations and people don't match up. For instance, you might expect:

- Your home group's leaders' input.
- A visit or direct contact from people in leadership.
- Your minister/vicar/pastor to be in direct contact frequently.
- Some recognition of your loss by the wider church fellowship, maybe at a service.
- Ministry prayer.
- To have follow-through pastorally.

- To be listened to and understood.
- Practical support.
- Prayer support.

Your list may include many different things. The point is, be realistic. However pastorally caring a church fellowship is, it's made up of fallible, busy humans who get it wrong! They give you space, thinking you need privacy – you want contact and reassurance you are loved. They allow close family/friends to minister – you know they're struggling deeply with their own grief as well as yours. They have busy lives in which your sadness is one small feature – you want to stop the world and shout out how much you are hurting!

Can you see how we have different perspectives? So what I'm saying is that Christians may let you down, often with the best of intentions, thinking they're doing the right thing. Sometimes, they'll let you down through sheer busyness and thoughtlessness. Rarely is it deliberate. So, I urge the bereaved person to be expansive in trying to believe the best. Try not to be over-demanding but realistic in your expectations of your fellow Christians. Forgive, forgive, forgive their ignorance and weaknesses. This way, any support you do receive will be a blessing and a bonus and you won't have to deal with your own unresolved issues and feelings of rejection. Concentrate on receiving the love from those God has placed alongside you and draw on this.

Also, by not focusing on people you're expecting things from means you'll notice the beautiful and unexpected surprises from the most unlikely people. I've already mentioned the lady who wrote faithfully to me over the months and years (my mum's minister's wife), even though she barely knew me. Then there were the letters from friends who were close to me in my late teens/early twenties – people who'd been part of my pre-marital life. I had wonderful letters and visits. Suddenly the years fell away and our busy 'grown-up' lives put momentarily on hold as we reconnected as friends, even though we were parted geographically.

Then nearer to home, there were many smaller blessings: flowers; a meal cooked; my freezer stocked up; people calling in; practical help; cartoons left in my school pigeon hole to make me laugh between teaching classes. If you focus on what you feel you should be receiving, you'll miss the love and support God is actually sending.

You know the story of the drowning Christian who, when a lifeboat and then a rescue helicopter arrive, refuses their assistance because he is waiting for God to rescue him. When he appears in heaven he asks God why he didn't rescue him. God points out that he sent a lifeboat and a helicopter! Don't be so narrowly focusing on one thing that you miss the wider picture. We must avoid being like this. You will discover gems, real jewels in the form of Christians. How can I be certain? Mainly because I know how committed God is to your welfare and if one person won't respond, he'll send another.

So some Christians misunderstand you. They'll make all sorts of wrong assumptions – they might even think you are wallowing in your situation when you cry in church. They don't know that music cuts through all your defences and allows God to minister directly to your heart. It might have been a really courageous act even getting to a service, knowing the pain would be revealed. But they don't know this.

I'll share a little from my own first-hand painful experience. We'd been part of a large city 'new' church for over five years. We'd led home groups, been involved in leadership and Geoff was part of a worship band. When I returned to church a couple of weeks after his death, I found it really difficult. Memories were everywhere, so were people. For me, worshipping God and coming into his presence with my broken heart meant the grief came to the surface.

Suddenly I no longer felt safe. I felt exposed and embarrassed. I forced myself to keep going, feeling that I 'should' but, finally, I had to admit that I just couldn't connect with the upbeat style of service at this time. I needed laments that acknowledged how ghastly life can be!

I now had a big decision to make and yet another change to face. As I live in a rural location, I'd been travelling half an hour to get to this 'alive' church. What alternatives did I have? I kept meeting with friends to pray and read the Bible until I felt ready to try a new church. Part of this was I didn't have to cope with people's pity. I could be anonymous in a new situation, sit at the back and exit swiftly if the emotion became too intense to be public. Eventually, I was able to stay longer and longer and without my friends' support. Then I began to accept prayer ministry. In this new Anglican church, those praying for me were amazingly sensitive. They prayed quietly, privately and on more than one occasion just cried with me. You know what? I sensed Jesus more at those moments than many others. It was like being given permission to grieve. There were no glib answers. No trite prayers, biblical quotations or triumphalist 'faith' statements – just genuine human empathy in the presence of the Divine. Such comfort came through this peaceful ministry with its absence of striving.

I eventually settled in my village Anglican church, a very different type of church from that of my previous experience but here I'm known as Kathy in my own right. I'm not seen as half of 'Kathy and Geoff'. No one responds to me as the 'tragic' widow. I find it refreshing.

I'm sharing my own pilgrimage but I would genuinely hope that you do not have to move church to find solace. I still wish I hadn't had to and that I'd been able to move through my grief in the place we loved and had served for so many years. I know I was misunderstood. I know when I stopped going people must have wondered why but no one asked, so I didn't get a chance to explain. I wish I'd had that opportunity. It hurt to be allowed to walk away with a broken heart and a desperate need for Christian love from the wider community. But, I thank God for my Christian friends who got me through this time. I recognise that many people just don't know how to deal with the grieving.

Tip: You want to express you care to a bereaved person in your fellowship. What can you do?

- *Do let them know if you've been praying.*
- *Don't ask them 'How are you?' unless you genuinely stay to listen and are prepared for the 'ugly side' of grief to show up.*
- *Do encourage them with a written card, meal or practical help.*
- *Don't be a 'rubbernecker' wanting to know the inside juicy details. It's not a spectator sport!*
- *Do offer to pray in person and be prepared to cry and listen.*
- *Don't offer trite platitudes or clichés. Better to say nothing at all.*

- *Do acknowledge their courage in facing church and a large group of people, when they feel so vulnerable. Just a quiet hand on the arm and a 'so good to see you' is all it takes. Don't let them cry alone. Move quietly alongside and offer a tissue or a hand on the arm but try not to draw others' attention to them. It's already embarrassing crying in public.*
- *Do go after someone who leaves in tears. Please don't ignore them just because it's in the middle of the prayers or sermon and you're embarrassed. Don't assume someone else will do it. They probably won't.*
- *Do make contact with a bereaved person, even after a few months. Don't assume others are doing it, they probably aren't.*
- *Do empathise. Don't pity.*
- *Do recognise tears come unexpectedly even after some years. Don't judge. It's not a competition to prove maturity as a Christian and 'get through grief quickly'.*
- *Do encourage, encourage, encourage. A kind word, a smile are both easy but they give solace.*
- *Despite some Christians believing they don't need to grieve because the loved one is saved, I have a suspicion the grief will arrive at a later date if it's not acknowledged when it happens.*

And remember
IT'S OK TO GRIEVE!

Even writing this chapter makes me feel vulnerable. I know some people might misinterpret the written word or misunderstand what I am saying. I hope not. I hope it will help people be real and not pretend, will help them make the most of a desperate situation and be true comforters to those who need them most.

Something quite unexpected happened as I was writing this chapter, which I think is a great illustration. I encourage birds to feed in my garden as I'm an avid lover of wildlife. Unfortunately, my dog came in to where I was working and, seeing the birds, he barked, frightening them away in all directions. A young greenfinch slapped straight into the window, landing on the slabs outside. I was mortified and the tears came quickly. It felt so unnecessary, this suffering, this death. It hadn't been killed outright but lay panting, wings outstretched, head on one side. I stood at the window, tears streaming down my face. Immediately, I was reminded of the verse in the Bible which says he cares even for the sparrows (Matthew 10:29). I found myself praying that God would take the little bird quickly and put it out of its misery (no, I couldn't do it myself!). I went out and gently moved it back into the undergrowth so it was a little sheltered.

A little while later I went to check and see if it had died. It was still there but its head had moved and it had tucked its wings in under its plumped-up feathers. Suddenly I felt hope. The next time I went to look it had flown off!

What an illustration of God's love. Firstly, I felt inordinate compassion for this tiny bird and its senseless suffering. Surely God feels this too, if we are created in his image (Genesis 1:26). Secondly, he heard my cry and noticed the suffering of a tiny bird. He hears our cries and prayers.

He knows when we are suffering and his love is moved to act. It might not be how we expect but it does come.

I never knew a heart could bear such pain
And survive
I never knew such searing tears would scar
But not win
Yet now
I can say
Yes, I can say
The heart receives its healing oil
The scars repair
And it can start to beat again
Though slowly
Steadily, until quickened once more
It starts to live again.

K.S. O'Brien

Chapter 11

Let's Get Real

> (A)LONE
> Alone is different
> From lonely
> Alone is complete – a(l)one
> Lonely misses
> Someone
> I am one
> But I turn l(one)ly
> Into a(l)one
> And I cope
>
> K.S. O'Brien

So what now? The immediacy of the death is behind you and, despite everything, you have continued to live. Some semblance of a normal life is beginning to unfold. You have now come to a place of acceptance of the death. Intense periods of grief are less and less. Tears still come but not in the unexpected, gut-wrenching way. You are moving forward. What does life and grief look like now?

On the way you'll have experienced the whole range of emotions – possibly anger, self-absorption, depression, hopelessness, sadness. Your road will have been unique to you yet part of the wider universal experience of humankind. You may still be experiencing sad days but you might also be wondering what lies ahead for you, without this person in your life.

One thing you'll already have realised. Most people have forgotten; forgotten the depth of your sadness and loss. Forgotten that you want to talk about the dead person and that it's healthy to do so. Forgotten that sometimes you still need to cry and forgotten that you might still be readjusting. So, tell them. If someone's being particularly insensitive, point it out to them. I've had to ask people to stop retelling the gory details of road accidents – they do it automatically – and remind them I've lived through it. Instead, if Christians, I direct them to pray for the families, knowing they'll need every shred of support possible. Be courageous and do likewise if you need to.

Special places may still bring sadness. Despite knocking down virtually all my skittles (as mentioned in a previous chapter) and facing our special places, there is one and only one that I haven't returned to. I'm not sure I ever will – maybe I will if in the future I am once more deeply in love. Somehow, that would help me face what is a unique place in my memory. I don't want it tarnished by my loss. At present, it's still a happy memory, a place we went on special occasions and had special times. But there shouldn't be many 'no go' areas. That would be unhealthy and too much of a tie to the past, so be careful.

There will also be times when you rush to share good news and are suddenly confronted, almost as if for the first time again, that they are dead. It happens.

If people forget, forgive them. If they no longer make allowances, take courage and heart from knowing God hasn't forgotten. I still meditate on my life verse, especially when having to take solo decisions which are hard to make.

'Be strong, vigorous and very courageous. Be not afraid, neither be dismayed for the Lord your God is with you wherever you go' (Joshua 1:9 AMP).

He promises to be with us in every decision.

> **Tip:** *Find verses for yourself which will inspire and give courage. I've listed a few below which will give you a start but find ones which are personal to you and bring you hope. (All references NIV.)*

And God will wipe away every tear from their eyes.

(Revelation 7:17)

The sovereign LORD will wipe away the tears from all faces.

(Isaiah 25:8)

'Come, let us return to the LORD.
He has torn us to pieces
   but he will heal us;
he has injured us
   but he will bind up our wounds. . . .

Let us acknowledge the LORD;
   let us press on to acknowledge him
As surely as the sun rises,
   he will appear;
he will come to us like the winter rains,
   like the spring rains that water the earth.'

(Hosea 6:1,3)

They will be like a well-watered garden,
   and they will sorrow no more. . . .

I will turn their mourning into gladness;
    I will give them comfort and joy instead of sorrow. . . .

    This is what the LORD says:
'Restrain your voice from weeping
    and your eyes from tears,
for your work will be rewarded,'
    declares the LORD. . . .
'So there is hope for your future,'
    declares the Lord.

(Jeremiah 31:12b–17a)

'May the LORD repay you for what you have done. May
you be richly rewarded by the LORD, the God of Israel,
under whose wings you have come to take refuge.'

(Ruth 2:12)

    I will lead her into the desert and speak tenderly to her.
There I will give her back her vineyards,
    and will make the Valley of Achor [trouble] a door of
    hope.
There she will sing as in the days of her youth . . .

(Hosea 2:14,15)

May the favour of the Lord our God rest upon us;
    establish the work of our hands for us –
    yes, establish the work of our hands.

(Psalm 90:17)

He tends his flock like a shepherd:
    He gathers the lambs in his arms
and carries them close to his heart;
    he gently leads those that have young.

(Isaiah 40:11 – the Messiah)

These were all commended for their faith, yet none of them received what had been promised.

(Hebrews 11:39)

'Be strong and courageous . . . Be strong and very courageous. . . . Have I not commanded you? Be strong and courageous. Do not be terrified; do not be discouraged, for the LORD your God will be with you wherever you go.'

(Joshua1:6–9)

Have mercy on me, O God, have mercy on me,
    for in you my soul takes refuge.
I will take refuge in the shadow of your wings
    until the disaster has passed.

I cry out to God Most High, to God who fulfils [his purpose] for me.

(Psalm 57:1,2)

Who is this coming up from the desert
    leaning on the arm of her lover?

(Song of Songs 8:5)

The righteous perish,
    and no-one ponders it in his heart;
devout men are taken away,
    and no-one understands
that the righteous are taken away
    to be spared from evil.
Those who walk uprightly
    enter into peace;
    they find rest as they lie in death.

(Isaiah 57:1,2)

In your day-to-day life, you're probably coping quite well with your grief but don't be surprised if occasionally your loss still hits you. I've found even over three years on, I'm impacted by seeing a road accident. It scares me. Recently, a car nearly drove into the back of me on the motorway. I had the dog (my friend Joy now has the other one) in the boot and I watched this car nearly ram into him! As I was near my exit, I managed to pull off swiftly but I fell apart, literally. I found myself shaking and tears were pouring down my face. It wasn't the fear of an accident or dying, it was the fear of losing the only thing left from my marriage with Geoff, the dog. We'd been together when he was born to our older dog. He means a tremendous amount to me and I couldn't face losing him too. I will, I know. Within five years he may no longer be alive but not just yet. . .

Again, as I'm writing, I've just put a CD on by Runrig. Haven't played it in a while and the first track is 'May Morning'. I skipped it! Geoff was killed in May, we played the track at his funeral and it still makes me cry. It's all about being vibrant and full of life when spring comes to Scotland. Too much pathos.

So, I make informed decisions, to minimise pain. Some days I can listen to such music, other times I can't. I make the choice. I fully believe in not dwelling on the things which make us sad.

Since Geoff died, I've retrained as a professional Life Coach, a profession which focuses on a person's potential and moving them towards fully realising this. Sometimes, I coach people who are not quite sure how to build a new life following a bereavement or divorce. They don't need grief counselling (or this has achieved its purpose) and they are now wanting help in moving forward and forging new lives.

One of the questions I often find myself asking is, 'What's the first thing you see when you go into your lounge?'

Often they will answer, 'A photo of X' the dead person. I will then ask them, 'How does it make you feel?' Immediately they invariably answer: 'Sad'.

At this point I will ask them, 'What is stopping you moving this photo to a different spot, one where you can choose when to look at it?'

This is a very simple illustration of the kind of thing we can do to help ourselves. Just because they are dead, we do not have to enshrine them. Photos can be moved out of direct eye-line. It's not a betrayal. As I have already said, I've placed all of mine on the stairs. I choose when to sit and look at them and mostly these days I pass without even noticing they are there. It's healthy. Of course, for others, having a photo out is exactly the right action for them. We're all different.

Another very real issue which people sometimes need to discover as they begin to rebuild their lives is, 'Who am I now?' We don't feel the same person. We're not. Depending on how close the dead person was to us, we have undergone changes. Some might be quite surprising.

I've found an adventurous spirit has risen up in me. I'm far more of a risk-taker than I'd realised. Geoff was naturally cautious and balanced that side of me but I find I'm enjoying pushing out my boundaries. It shows itself in clothes, in decisions, in travel, in my business life, in my creativity and unwillingness to conform to the norm.

I am not the person Geoff was married to. I've changed. I'm much more self-reliant and resilient. What about you? What have you learned to do as a result of this death? How has it changed you?

Some of you will be saying, but I haven't changed and I don't have the inner resources needed to change. I still need my loved one! I can't cope without them.

You might – but sadly, they are not here however much you need them, so you will have to develop a coping strategy. There is a way forward, even if you've allowed yourself to become a bit stuck in looking backwards. There's a transition time where you look backwards and forwards at the same time. We can't always jump forwards without looking back to where we've come from.

However, if your life consists of reliving the past and only relating backwards, I would suggest that you need to start building for your own future. Start being honest and asking yourself some questions:

- *What would you like to do that would move you forward?*
- *What would it take to help you move towards this?*
- *What new interest could you take up? Is there an old one that you've put to one side?*
- *What is stopping you from moving through your grief?*
- *Is there anything in your home which makes you feel sad, rather than bringing a smile, which is connected to the dead person? What are you going to do to change this situation? (Remember I had these pictures which made me sad and I didn't realise it. I've never missed them because I have other things which remind me of Geoff and bring a smile.)*

Rebuilding takes time and sometimes you do need someone, like a good friend or a Christian coach, alongside you. It does take time to readjust and I'm not someone who believes you 'get over' grief or that you need 'healing'. It's a process and, fourteen years on, there are moments when I really miss my dad. On a star-lit night, I wish I could now, as an adult, tell him how much I appreciate the love of the outdoors and nature which he instilled in me. As a teenager I would never acknowledge how much it meant. I wish I could rectify that. I can't, but I can be thankful for the gift he gave me of excitement, adventure and love of nature.

And remember, there's no rush, there's no schedule but your own. The only thing to do is – keep moving forward. If you find you've insecurities which are holding you back, do this simple exercise:

> *Imagine yourself at the end of your life, looking back over it. Are you content? Are there things you wish you'd done but didn't? How will you feel if you remain in your grieving? What will you regret not having done?*

Now go and put one thing in place towards doing it. Then, you will be moving on and the gift of their love will still be with you. You will be honouring their life and their desire for you to be happy and go on living. Above all, you will be honouring your life, given by God for purposes only he has designed especially for you (Jeremiah 29:11).

I wish you every joy and blessing on this journey. It's one you don't have to travel alone. My prayer is that this book has blessed you and will continue to do so. Pray you'll reach the place I now find myself in, reading about Geoff's death as though it happened to someone else. The words in my diary no longer feel like my life – I've moved on. It happened to another Kathy, a different one, a long, long time ago: a different life and a different world. I pray that you, too, may come through whole and content.

Chapter 12

Prayers

These prayers are designed merely as a starting point for when you don't know how to pray. I hope they will start you on deeper conversations with God the Father, and bring comfort when you really need it. (Note that there's a prayer for those who may be concerned over the deceased's eternal destiny, in Chapter 9.)

Prayer for releasing confusion and anger:

> *Lord, I am angry and confused. I barely know which way to turn. I'm angry with people, with circumstances, with my loved one (insert their name) and sometimes I'm angry with you God. Please help me not to feel victimised or to point a finger of blame because I'm angry. Help me to let go of anger safely. Please don't let me hurt others because I am hurting. In the midst of this pain and turmoil will you comfort me with your presence? When people let me down, will you help me to believe the best of them and where necessary to truly forgive? Thank you. Amen.*

Prayer for someone struggling with anger and bitterness:

> *Dear Lord, I'm struggling with such strong emotions. I'm angry and bitter. The bitterness seems to want to consume me but I know it's wrong and I'm sorry. Please will you forgive me and stop this bitterness from taking root in my life. Remind me when I slip into talking negatively about the situation and the people involved. Save me from myself. People have let me down so badly. What do I do with all this anger? Show me the right way to react. I truly don't want to give bitterness and wrongful anger any place in my life but to respond as you would respond. I know it is unhealthy emotionally and spiritually to remain bitter and angry. Please help me. Thank you that you hear my heart cry to be forgiving and to let it go. Amen.*

Prayer for someone struggling with fear and loneliness:

> *Dear Lord, I am so lonely and so often afraid. Please come close and comfort me. You say that your 'perfect love drives out fear' (1 Jn. 4:18). When I forget, will you remind me of that 'perfect love' you have for me. When fear tries to overwhelm, let your words of comfort fill my mind, for you've said that if I 'make the Most High' my 'dwelling' then 'no harm will befall' me and that you will protect me (Ps. 91). I'm sorry that I so often forget that I am not truly alone, that you have sent the Holy Spirit to comfort me and to watch over me. Thank you. Amen.*

Suggestion: Have Psalm 91 close to hand, so you can read it when you are frightened.

Are you struggling to forgive? Perhaps someone has been less than sensitive to your loss, or there are other reasons why you feel it is almost impossible to forgive somebody. Here is a prayer for those who are struggling to forgive:

> *Dear Lord, I need to be honest with you, I'm strug-gling to forgive. Everything within me wants to carry on blaming (name of person). I find myself not even wanting to forgive them. Yet, you make it so clear that if I don't forgive, you are not able to forgive me. Lord, at this point I choose to forgive (name of person) for (name action) and I pray that you will release the feel-ings as a direct result of my choice. I pray that you will bless them. Amen.*

Older people often have a very hard time when their loved ones die. So here is a prayer for the elderly to say:

> *Dear Lord, I am lost. My whole life has been turned upside down by (insert loved one's name) death. There are days when I just don't think I can go on. Please will you show me that my life still counts; that you have purposes for the remainder of my life and that people still need and love me. When I want to give up, will you help me to adjust and give me the courage I need to go on? Thank you. Amen.*

Prayer for those who are struggling with an elderly rela-tive who doesn't want to move on:

> *Lord, I need you. I'm sometimes at my wits end. Since (loved one's name) died (the elderly person's name) just doesn't seem to want to go on. I love them but I need help. I commit them to your care and ask that you will give me the wisdom to know what I can and what I can't do. Help me to know when to seek out additional help myself and remind me to be loving and kind in all that I do, however overwhelmed I am feeling. Please bless them and help them to want to still embrace all that life has. Thank you. Amen.*

Prayer for someone who has lost a child:

> *Lord, my heart is broken. A part of me died when (name of the child) died. How can I bear this pain? I didn't know that a heart could bear so much pain and survive. I need your comfort to keep going but I also want to thank you for the short time I had with (name of the child). Help me to remember the good times, however brief. I believe that you will provide all the strength that I will need in the coming days to get through this dark valley. Thank you that you promise to be strong when I feel weak. Thank you for being there and crying with me, in the midst of my grief. Amen.*

(*Emily, a Child in Heaven* by Deborah Lycett, is a book written specifically about stillbirth. Published 2004, Authentic Lifestyle.)

Prayer for someone who has lost somebody through suicide:

> *Dear Lord, (name of person) is dead and I am reeling, not knowing what to think or feel. I'm overwhelmed with strong emotions and a desperate feeling that I should have done something. Lord, please comfort me. Please help me come to terms with what has happened. I've no idea whether (name of person) is with you but I want to commit them into your care, trusting that you know a person's heart much better than anyone and that you love everyone. Please help me to pick up the pieces of my life and not to let this overshadow my remaining years. Help me to forgive myself for not being able to help them. Where I am hurting, please touch my emotions and comfort me and for all those who have been impacted by (name of person) death, I pray that you will draw near to them also. Thank you. Amen.*

If you find yourself struggling with what has been termed 'survivor guilt' after the death of a loved one, whether you have lost them through a tragic accident, to illness or suicide, you might want to talk it through with someone who will understand. This might be a friend or family member. Alternatively, contact one of the organisations listed in the Appendix for additional support.

Prayer for those dealing with impending death of a loved one/having suffered a long time watching someone close to them die:

> *Dear Lord, please be really close to us. I'm exhausted, mentally, physically and even spiritually. It's been so hard watching (name of loved one) suffer and I want*

> *them to be set free from this awful pain. Yet, I'm scared too. I love them and don't want that final moment to come. Please come close to us all. Help us to say all our 'goodbyes' and 'I love yous'. Help us to create precious memories that will sustain us once (name of loved one) has died. I will need you to be very close, to guard my heart from blaming you for this suffering. Remind me that you care about this pain; that you are here with us in it all. Please don't let any of us who love (name of loved one) become bitter towards you. Sustain us all with your grace whatever may happen. In Jesus' name I ask. Thank you. Amen.*

Prayer to pray for children of the bereaved:

> *Dear Lord, I ask you to come close and comfort the children of (name of loved one). They are deeply shocked and grieving at the moment. I pray that you will protect and guard them throughout this ordeal. Hide them away from the enemy who would seek to harden their hearts towards you. Will you comfort them deeply, so that they know you really do care about them and their pain? I pray that throughout their years you will send people to help them, to love them, to minister to them, so that your love will sustain them at every turn. Thank you that you care even more than I do for their long-term welfare. Please look after them. Amen.*

Prayer for the person who may have 'caused' the death:

> *Dear Lord, this is a prayer I struggle to pray but know that I need to. Please be with (name of person who 'caused' the death). You alone know what they too are struggling with and facing as a result of this death. I forgive them, totally, for their involvement in (name of loved one)'s death and choose not to let any bitterness grow in my heart towards them. As a result, I pray that you will bless them abundantly and draw near to them at this time, revealing your love to them too. Amen.*

Throughout this book, I have constantly referred to my faith in Jesus, to the personal relationship I have with him that has sustained me through everything. Not only has it sustained me but it has provided my life with purpose, a meaning, a direction and a fulfilling joy – both before and after Geoff's death. Beyond that is the wonderful expectation of eternity spent not only with Jesus but reunited with Geoff and many other Christians. If you would like to experience this wonderful relationship and reassurance, then I invite you to pray the following prayer of commitment.

Prayer of commitment:

> *Dear Jesus, I recognise that I do not yet know you but I want to. I would like to commit my life into your hands, to ask you to come and take control of it as my Lord. I am sorry for the wrong things I have done and now choose to turn away from them, asking you to forgive me. I understand and believe that when you died on the cross, you were taking the punishment I*

deserve for all the wrong things I have said and done to hurt you and others. Please come into my life and fill me with your Holy Spirit. Help me to grow into maturity as a Christian. Thank you. Amen.

Finally, here are two prayers that I pray for you who are bereaved, and who have a loved one who is bereaved:

Dearest Lord Jesus, my Friend and my Saviour: I pray for each person who picks up this book and who reads any part of it. I pray that you will speak to them directly, that you will bring comfort and reassurance. I pray that you will draw near to them and give them hope when they are in the very darkest times. God of comfort, provide your comfort to them. God who knows every hair of our heads, every tear that we cry, comfort your people and draw them closer to you; that your glory may be revealed to them and the total reassurance of the life to come. Thank you. Amen.

Prayer for friends and family of a bereaved person:

Dear Lord, I pray that this book will be a tool in the hands of those seeking to help. I pray that when they find themselves unsure of what to do, that the right page will open up for them, the right Tip, the right example. Grant them courage and grace to provide support at this time and thank you for them. Thank you that they are willing to help, when many turn away. Please bless them abundantly as they give out to those who need them. Thank you. Amen.

Where, O death, is your victory?
Where, O death, is your sting?

(1 Corinthians 15:55)

Places to Find Additional Help

Cruse Bereavement Care: 126 Sheen Road, Richmond, Surrey, TW9 1UR.
Helpline: 0870 167 1677
Cruse offers personal and professional help to the bereaved. There is a specialist service for children (twelve to eighteen years) Freephone 0808 808 1677.
www.crusebereavementcare.org.uk

The WAY Foundation: PO Box 74, Penarth, CF64 5ZD.
Please enclose an SAE.
Tel: 0870 011 3450
www.wayfoundation.org.uk
Email: wayfoundation@compuserve.com
Widowed and Young is a group providing support and social interaction for those who have been widowed young.

New Directions Life Coaching (UK): Kathy O'Brien's Life Coaching business, where she specialises in coaching people to realise their potential and live fulfilling lives.
www.newdirectionslifecoaching.co.uk.

healingpool e hotmail . co. uk

The Samaritans: Look under S in your local phone directory. They offer a 24-hour listening and befriending service.

SOBS: Survivors of Bereavement by Suicide. Centre 88, Saner Street, Hull, HU3 2TR.
Helpline: 0870 241 3337 (9am–9pm).
www.uk-sobs.org.uk_

SCARD: Support and Care After Road Death. PO Box 62, Brighouse, West Yorkshire, HD6 3YY.
Helpline 01484 401622 for the bereaved and injured only (9 a.m.–9 p.m.) Other inquiries ring 01484 384 702 (office hours).
www.scard.org.uk

Macmillan Cancer Relief: Cancerline 0808 808 2020 (Mon–Fri 9 a.m.–6 p.m.).
www.cancerlink.org
Information and support service for anyone affected by cancer. Acts as a resource to cancer support and self-help groups throughout the UK, and produces a range of publications about cancer.

For Christian Singles and Those Wanting Friendships

Christian Connection: Christian website for widening friendships and relationships. UK only.
www.christianconnection.co.uk

The Network: An association for single Christians. PO Box 20, Braunton, Devon, EX33 2YX. Tel: 01271 817 093.
www.singleandchristian.co.uk

Other Titles in the

Hope for the Hurting Series

EMILY: A CHILD IN HEAVEN

Emily: A Child in Heaven is a deeply moving account of loss. The author's second child, Emily, was stillborn. While Deborah Lyycett details her loss, grief and deepest emotions, *Emily: A Child in Heaven* is an exceptionally well balanced account of personal tragedy.

Throughout the book is an underpinning of the author's strong faith in God despite her personal tragedy, and she offers comfort and hope for anyone who has been similarly bereaved.

1-86024-443-2 ● £5.99

HIDDEN HUNGER

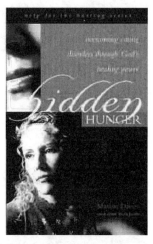

Food is personal. It touches on issues which are personal, even intimate – your likes and dislikes, comforts and cravings, family history, home life, and social life. This is a book about problems related to food.

Although eating problems are very real, they're actually the symptons of a much deeper hunger, which is usually hidden – even from those who are desperate to be free.

Maxine Davies knows about struggles with eating and appetite. This book tells her story and how she overcame those struggles.

Her desire is that this book will shed light on the subject of eating disorders and leave you with a sense of hope for the future.

1-86024-296-0 ● £4.99